To Lian...

Wishing you happiness always.

Anne

+

EARTH ANGEL

Anne Bulcraig

Earth Angel

ISBN 978-0-9569018-0-4

Published by
High Spirits Publishing
Bognor Regis
West Sussex
PO22 9LX

email: anne.psi@sky.com
www.anne-psychicmedium.co.uk

A CIP catalogue record of this book
can be obtained from the British Library.

Book designed by Michael Walsh at
The Better Book Company • 5 Lime Close •
Chichester PO19 6SW

and printed by ImprintDigital.net
Seychelles Farm, Upton Pyne, Exeter Devon EX5 5HY

This book is a true and accurate account of the life, experiences and recollections of the author.

Views and opinions expressed are solely of the author. Some names have been changed to respect the privacy of others.

Dedications

To my wonderful nan, Malvina McKay, I have always felt your unconditional love. Thank you for being there for me in life and death.

To my amazing dad, Frederick Wood. I only wish I had noticed how bright your light shone whilst you were on Earth.

To my husband, Andy. Your constant support and love means the world to me. Thank you for everything.

And to my incredible friend, Vince. You taught me to always reach for the stars. I promise you that I won't stop trying ...

Contents

Prologue

March 5th 1999.

Oh my God! I take a sneaky nip out of my hip flask, glancing round to make sure that no one has noticed. They haven't; they're all too busy preparing their tables for the evening.

Nervously I pick up the rose-quartz crystal I've just purchased and squeeze it tightly between my sweaty palms. Jo at the crystal stall assured me it would settle my nerves. It doesn't seem to be working too well.

'Please be with me tonight, you lot,' I mutter repeatedly.

As I watch the assortment of tarot readers, psychics and mediums laugh and joke with each other as they prepare for the evening ahead, I wonder what on earth I'm doing sitting here pretending to be one of them. They all look so professional, so confident, so flipping serene and spiritual. I feel like a fake. I want to go and hide behind the aloe vera stall with my husband Andy. Better still, go and lock myself in the toilets for the night, but it's too late to back out now...

It's fifteen minutes to show time!

One of the readers arrives late and hurries over to the empty table next to me, eager to set up before the public arrives. It's Minnie, a very popular tarot reader. Her usual purple robes swish around as she unpacks her tablecloth and bits and pieces.

I glance down at myself. Hmm, maybe my pink Bag-puss T-shirt was a bit of a mistake.

'Hi, Anne!' Minnie sings in her usual cheerful tone. Suddenly she stops setting up her table and turns her full attention to me. 'What are you doing? Why aren't you at the aloe vera stall?'

'I'm reading today,' I mutter sheepishly.

Minnie's almost black eyes pop open in amazement. 'You? Reading? But you're not a psychic! You shouldn't run before you can walk, sweetheart!' With a toss of her wild black hair, Minnie turns away and continues in silence to set-up, throwing me the occasional dark look.

In a way, I can't blame Minnie. I can see I've had quite a few baffled looks from the other ten readers around the hall. For the past year-and-a-half I've been attending the psychic fairs with Andy, selling health and beauty products. Now suddenly, I'm sitting here on a small table of my own, with just my lamp and a few crystals for company, proclaiming to be a reader!

No wonder the others are puzzled. I've never even mentioned to anyone that it's always been my dream to work for Spirit. Until this moment I honestly thought the chances of it happening were so remote, there was more chance of me becoming the next Prime Minister of Great Britain.

But Spirit had other ideas...

A tall blond man in his fifties approaches my table. It's Roger. 'All right, Anne?' he asks kindly. 'You look a bit shaky, love!'

I nod. 'I'm okay, thanks.'

He sits down and takes my hand. 'I just wanted to wish you luck. You know, Anne, you're as good as anyone here. Don't forget that, okay? You'll be fantastic.' He gets up, gives me a wink and goes back to his table.

A massive lump forms in my throat. He'll never know how much those few simple words will mean to me. Another reader, Julie, comes over and presses something in my hand. 'For courage and strength,' she whispers, and then slips away. It's a tiny slither of light blue crystal; I don't know what it's called, but that doesn't matter. I do find strength, but not from the crystal, from her kindness.

I glance at the clock. Five minutes to show time!

Carol is doing her usual rounds smudging the hall with some evil smelling concoction, which supposedly clears the air of negative energy. The overpowering whiff has me reaching for my asthma inhaler.

Pete, the fair organiser, is chiming some Chinese clearing bells. The sound is quite soothing and somehow calms me a little. The CD player is wafting out some new age track – all moody drums and mystic chanting.

The scene is set. All that's needed are the 'punters' as most of the readers call the public.

Tinkle of coins at the door alert me that the first people have arrived, and are staring round expectantly at the array of stalls and readers. I find myself praying for a meteor to come crashing down. Just outside the hall of course, as I wouldn't want anyone to be hurt, only distracted. A few minutes pass, but no sign of the meteor! The three elderly women are drawing closer to my table. I realise that I'll have to make my own plans for escape.

The toilets!

My face is bright red and my chest and neck has broken out in its usual nervous rash. I splash cold water on my face and stare angrily at my reflection. *Get a grip, Anne! This is what you want, isn't it? I can do this. I know I can. I've got to do it!*

But maybe Minnie's right! I've never sat in circle. I've never been to any psychic development class or group. I don't even have a clue how to read a palm or tarot cards like the others. God, I don't even know all the flipping astrology signs!

Maybe I'm just kidding myself I can do this. Am I ready to be let loose on the public? I'm thirty years old, not very young, but the youngest reader here. They've all had so much more experience than me. I close my eyes as I battle with myself and am suddenly aware of my friends from Spirit around me.

You'll be fine! I hear in my head.

I wait to hear any more great words of inspiration from 'That Lot Upstairs', but as nothing is forthcoming, I slowly make my way back to my table. To my horror, one of the elderly women is sitting there, obviously waiting for me.

'Hello dear, the lady at the door said you're doing readings for five pounds today. Is that right?'

'Yes. This is my first day,' I explain. 'So if you're happy to be my guinea pig...'

She stares critically at me for a second, and then breaks into a smile, plonking a fiver into my sweaty hand. 'Let's give it a go, shall we?' I quickly put the money to one side. I dare not take it in case it jinxes the reading.

'I'm after contact with the other side,' she tells me.

'I'll do my best,' I say, silently yelling at my guides for help. They don't let me down. Within seconds, I'm strongly aware of a man standing next to me. I don't see him with my physical eyes, but all the same, I know he's there.

I describe him and tell her I could hear him saying that he's called Jim.

'It's my husband,' she says in wonder. I don't know who is more surprised – her or me! This man draws so close to me I can literally feel the love he has for his wife. He gives me many facts about her and her family, which she can verify. The reading lasts around half-an-hour, and in that time I'm so focused the meteor I'd wished for earlier could've crashed outside, and I wouldn't have noticed.

After the reading, she says she can't thank me enough that I've put her mind at rest about her beloved Jim.

When she's gone, I pop outside to take a breather. I'm on such a high! It's the most wonderful exhilarating feeling in the world. I stare up at the evening sky and notice how bright the stars look. It's like I've been wandering around with tunnel vision, and now suddenly everything is in sharp focus.

Back at my table, a young man in his twenties approaches, grinning sheepishly at me. 'Give us a reading,' he says. 'I don't believe in all this mumbo-jumbo, but my other half is well in to it. I'll give it a go for a fiver. All the others are charging thirty smackaroonies!'

I smile weakly, not liking the idea of having a sceptic thrust upon me so quickly.

Actually, the reading goes quite well. Nothing to set the world on fire, and nowhere as good as the elderly lady, but I manage to pick up some good solid stuff; mostly about his work and relationship. His granddad makes a very short appearance, but soon disappears when it becomes apparent the young guy isn't too fussed about the 'dead dudes'! It's really more of a psychic read, but that's fine. I watch him re-join his girlfriend at the crystal stall, chattering away animatedly as he points me out.

Nine readings later and I've never felt so utterly shattered in my life.

The crowds have thinned out and there's only a few people left, finishing off their readings. Pete strolls over to collect my table rent. I give him half of the forty-five pounds I've taken. This is what we've agreed before the fair. The other readers pay a set fee of sixty-five pounds.

'Well, young lady, all the reports we've had about you have been excellent this evening, so I'm happy to offer you a regular table if you'd like. The only thing is a couple of the readers don't like you undercutting them, so you'll have to charge thirty quid from now on.'

I nod, still feeling giddy from the success of the evening.

'I'd really like to do a few more,' I say, wondering what I'm letting myself in for...

1

Early Experiences

People often asked me if I was psychic when I was a child, but my childhood wasn't as eventful as you might expect. I know many mediums, when recalling their early memories will have plenty of stories to tell of playing alongside spirit children. But I can't say this was true for me. It would've been very nice as I had quite a lonely childhood, but unfortunately I don't remember any 'imaginary friends'.

The very first strange experience that I recall occurred when I was nine. It's the most vivid childhood memory I have, and when you hear it I think you will understand why.

As a child I adored arts and crafts and spent many hours drawing pictures and making various collages with bits of material my nan used to save for me from her odds and sods box.

It was Easter and I'd spent the morning drawing and colouring an Easter card for my mum. I really wanted it to be special. My family had had an awful year, as my older brother Rick and his wife Diane had been involved in a horrific motorbike accident a few months previously.

Also, Mum had been quite poorly, so I put loads of love and care into the card. I vividly remember the colourful egg on the front, and the red and green glitter I'd glued on it. I couldn't wait to give it to Mum. I was so pleased with it, and knew she'd love it, but before I could hand it over to her, Mum and I had a huge argument.

In writing this, I've tried to remember what triggered this argument, but I honestly don't know. It was probably over something silly – as most arguments are.

I stormed to my room, took the card from its hiding place, and ripped it clean in half, then promptly rushed off to find Nan. Nan and Granddad lived upstairs, and if ever I was upset, Nan was always the one I sought out for comfort.

Three custard creams (Nan's favourite) later, and a chat from my wise nan, I was feeling deeply ashamed and sorry for upsetting Mum, and for destroying the card I'd put so much care into making for her.

Coming downstairs, I could hear Mum sobbing quietly in the lounge. I crouched on the stairs and willed with all my heart for the card to mend itself. Exactly what I said or did I'm not completely sure, but I vividly remember *willing* the card to be whole again.

As I sat there, this incredibly powerful feeling shot through me. The card *would* be whole again. It *would*. No question, no argument, it just WOULD!

I sprung up, rushed to my room, and there it was – *as fresh as when I'd made it*! Strangely, I remember that this didn't surprise me in the slightest. In fact, I would've been more shocked if it *hadn't* been whole.

I'm very apprehensive about telling people about this amazing experience, because I realised that it sounds so far-fetched. All I can say is that it *did* happen.

Years later, I asked my spirit mates how the card had miraculously fixed itself, but all I got for my trouble was an enigmatic smile...

The only other paranormal memory I have as a child is of a dream I had that came true.

I'm very aware that our spirit friends will often use dreams as a way of communicating with us. They'll also sometimes use our dreams to impress us with a future event. This is what happened to me when I was about ten or eleven.

I had this very vivid dream about a carpet. Yes, a carpet! Hardly a very spiritual object, I can see what you're thinking, and you're right. And no, I'm not going to tell you that this turned out to be a Magic Carpet that I used to fly on to school!

In my dream my Uncle Ronnie turned up at our house with this dishwater grey and red patterned carpet. Uncle Ronnie had carried it in my bedroom and rolled it out. Even in the dream I remember saying, 'Yuck! Hope we don't have to keep it, it's awful!' But Mum had insisted that it was perfect, and it was staying whether I liked it or not. Then I woke up.

A few days later Uncle Ronnie turned up with his usual cheeky grin. He told Mum he'd brought over a few things he thought might be useful.

My mouth fell open in absolute disbelief as Uncle Ronnie started to unroll the carpet. It was the *exact* hideous carpet I'd dreamt about.

'That'll be fine in Anne's room,' Mum said happily.

We had that awful carpet for about four or five years, and every time I looked at it I wondered how on earth I could've seen a carpet in a dream that had materialised in real life a few days later! Spirit had obviously seen this carpet and super-imposed the dream into my subconscious mind.

Of course the dream itself wasn't important. I realise now that Spirit was trying to make me *think,* and wonder how this come-true dream had happened. When my 'egg card' incident had happened, I'd just accepted it unquestioningly, but I was older now and wanted to understand how this dream had been possible. I started to read books on premonitions and other paranormal subjects. My friends used to tease me relentlessly, but I was desperately searching for answers.

The journey had begun...

When I was ten, Mum told me a story from her childhood that intrigued me.

Mum had been twelve when she'd become extremely ill with meningitis. She was virtually on her deathbed. Being Catholic she'd even had the last rites. Mum told me that she remembered being alone in this small hospital room, when suddenly, to her astonishment, the wall slowly dissolved revealing a beautiful garden. In the garden many children were playing happily together.

Mum explained to me that the colours she saw in the garden were different to any colours she'd ever seen in her life, and were so incredibly vivid it looked as if everything had an 'inner-light'.

A little girl of about five skipped into the hospital room and handed Mum a posy of beautiful flowers. She told Mum not to worry because she would soon get better. Then, waving, she disappeared back into the garden.

The next day Mum's condition stabilised, and in the following days she made a 'miraculous recovery'. When Mum told *her* mum about the girl and the garden, and described the girl, my nan showed her a photo of Pam, my mum's cousin, who'd died the previous year. Mum had never seen this cousin when she was alive, and was amazed to realise that it was the *same* girl who'd given her the flowers, and had predicted her recovery!

To this day, over sixty years later, Mum hasn't changed her recollection of this amazing incident – and I've asked her about it often enough. I believe that Mum had a 'near-death experience'. She was so close to passing over that she was able to see and interact with the Spiritual Realms. This experience seemed to 'open up' Mum to psychic activity, and throughout her life she's had many strange incidents occur.

As a teenager, my biggest spiritual influence was my older brother, Rick. He and his wife, Diane, were involved with the local Spiritualist church. As a curious thirteen-year-old, I was totally fascinated by the stories he and Diane used to tell me. I wondered how it could be possible to receive messages from dead people. Rick was very patient with me, and spent hours answering my questions and talking to me about his personal beliefs.

I listened in awe as he explained in a very simple way that when you died a part of you, your Spirit, your Soul, whatever you wanted to call it, went to another place.

He called this place 'The Summerlands'. To my mind, it seemed an idyllic place, full of joy and laughter, and seemed to describe the very place Mum had seen when she'd had her near-death experience. Rick also used to scare me with a place called 'The Dark-Lands', where, according to him, nasty people ended up! But as Rick explained, even if they'd been *very* bad, they still had a chance to redeem themselves by learning compassion and helping others. Of course, since those days, I've learnt that there is *much* more to these lands than Rick described, but at the time, it was enough to keep me intrigued. I desperately yearned to learn as much as possible about these amazing places.

One day, after a particularly deep chat with Rick, I decided that I wanted to go and see for myself what really went on in this mysterious Spiritualist church.

I spent weeks nagging my best mate, Michelle, to accompany me. In the end she reluctantly agreed. Secretly, I think she was as curious as me.

My legs wobbled slightly as we entered the inconspicuous building set behind a row of shops, a short walk from my house. Michelle was chattering away as usual (no change there, thirty years on), but I couldn't concentrate on her words. Somehow I sensed that this evening would be of great importance to me.

Looking around for a seat, I noticed the youngest person there was at least sixty! Michelle was pulling at my arm, trying her hardest to drag me back out, but I was determined that now we were actually here we were *staying*. We took our seats, but then had to stand to sing a hymn.

Instead of singing, Michelle scrabbled about in her handbag, pulled out a bag of sweets and threw me one. The grey-haired lady frowned down at us from the tiny platform. I could almost see the thought-bubble over her head, saying, '*This isn't a cinema, you know*!'

The lady in front of us belted out the hymn as if her life depended on it. Along with her gusty singing, and the sweet-faced organist, who was plonking away with every other note off-key, Michelle started to pull agonised expressions, pressing her palms over her ears.

That was it. I got the giggles! We were cracking up, whilst the iron-haired lady on the platform was giving us absolute daggers. The harder I tried to stop laughing, the more it bubbled over. Even when the hymn was over and everyone was seated again, we couldn't seem to calm ourselves. To this day, I can't believe we weren't kicked out! If we *had* been I wonder if my life would've taken a completely different path. I doubt it, but you never know.

Once the medium, a smartly dressed man, stood up and started his demonstration, giggling was the furthest thing from my mind. I can't recall the exact content of his messages, but I *do* clearly remember that the information he was giving was obviously hitting home with the people he was calling on.

The thing that struck me the most was the genuine comfort and joy they seemed to be receiving from this quietly spoken man. I clearly remember him linking with a tiny elderly gentleman in the seat across the aisle from us.

The medium linked with the man's wife, and I watched in fascination as this dejected gentleman came to life as message after message was passed on to him from her. His watery eyes lit up with genuine happiness, and he sat up straight in his chair, laughing and joking at long forgotten memories the medium was relating from his wife. After the reading, the elderly chap told the medium that he simply didn't have words to express his thanks for bringing his 'old girl' back to him. He said how much peace it'd given him to know she was fine. Michelle had to hand me a tissue I was sniffing so much. (Must've been my allergies playing up!)

After I'd witnessed this miraculous three-way exchange between the elderly gentleman, his late wife and the medium, I was totally sure of one thing – *this* was what I wanted to do.

At school, I decided to try to get some guidance on what I'd experienced at the church.

Most of my friends wanted to be either hairdressers or travel agents, but I wanted to talk to dead people. Fine! What would the school careers adviser make of that one?

Mr Morris, our religious education teacher, was a gentle, kindly soul, so I decided to have a word with him. After class, I plucked up the courage and approached his desk. I wanted to ask him a few questions regarding my visit to the Spiritualist church. Big mistake!

'Can I speak to you for a minute, please, Mr Morris?' I asked shyly. 'I'm a bit confused about religion and stuff.'

Mr Morris smiled encouragingly at me. 'Ask away, Anne. That's what I'm here for.'

'Well, I was just wondering what you thought about spiritualist mediums?' I blurted out. 'You know, people who talk to the dead.'

Mr Morris's eyes widened and he looked so shocked I though he was going to cross himself. He stared at me, agog, for what seemed like ages. Finally, he almost yelled words at me that I've never forgotten! 'These so-called mediums are *very* dangerous people, Anne. You *mustn't* dabble with the dead. It's *wrong*! These charlatans who prey on the vulnerable are nothing short of *evil*! And anyone who gets involved in such *darkness* is just as bad.'

I must admit I wasn't sure what I was expecting, but his strong reaction shook me up. Why was it bad to bring comfort and peace to people? How could it be *evil*?

What made Mr Morris so sure anyway? My mind pictured the medium from the church. He certainly didn't *look* evil. And as for the elderly gentleman, he just wanted to reach his beloved 'old girl'. What was wrong with that? It didn't make any sense.

To a shy thirteen-year-old, the word *evil* is pretty strong, and I admit that after my little chat with the so-called expert on the After-life I almost changed my mind about becoming a medium.

Almost...

Four years later, I was rummaging through an old pile of books at a jumble sale, when I spotted a book by Doris Stokes called *Voices in my Ear*. Excitedly I took it home and sat up all night reading it. What an amazing lady! It immediately sparked up my old interest in spiritual things.

At the time I was seventeen and at six-form college. Michelle and I used to both waitress evenings and weekends at the local Wimpy bar to earn money for our beloved clubbing holidays abroad, usually Ibiza. It was on one of our wild nights out that I gave my very first reading...

Lost in my own world as I twirled around the dance floor, a spiky-haired guy suddenly grabbed my hands and started dancing with me. After a while, he said he wanted a chat, so we went to the bar to get a drink. I must admit I was a bit tipsy – but definitely not drunk!

We were chatting away, with a fair amount of flirting going on, as you do when you're a teenager on holiday. He told me that he was from London and was twenty. Whilst he was chatting away, I suddenly had this overwhelming sense of a woman standing by us. I didn't see her with my eyes, but I *knew* she was there.

This was quite literally the first time in my life I'd had this sensation, and it's very hard to explain how it feels. I thought I was imagining her, so of course I just ignored her.

'So what do you do?' the guy asked, sipping his drink.

'Err, I'm at college.'

Ruth, Ruth, Ruth... the female voice in my head chanted.

'Ruth,' I repeated aloud. 'Who's Ruth?'

His eyes widened. 'Ruth's my sister, but how do you know that?' It was a fair question.

'Is she dead?' I ventured cautiously.

'I bloody hope not!' The poor guy was starting to look slightly agitated, which, looking back, was understandable! 'What are you on about?'

It was then that the 'floodgates' opened.

I started to describe the woman I was sensing standing by our side. When I'd finished, he told me that his mum had died the previous year, and he completely understood the details I'd given him.

The whole process felt incredibly natural to me. Whenever I'd passed on some information, there was yet more information pouring into my mind from this lady. She seemed desperate to let her son and daughter know that she was okay, and was still very much with them.

The guy was a total emotional wreck when his friends finally led him away; no doubt wondering what on earth I'd done to the poor bloke! I never saw him again, but wondered if he ever had the nerve to chat anyone up after that evening with me!

Back at the hotel, I couldn't *believe* what'd just occurred. I actually ended up convincing myself that he'd just agreed with the information I was giving him just to keep me chatting to him. Yes, that's what must have happened. There couldn't be any other explanation, could there?

But deep down, when I remembered the look on his face, I knew he'd been truly shocked.

Over the next two or three years I drove my friends crazy. Every time we went on a girl's night out, I would end up given some poor unsuspecting guy a 'reading'. Michelle used to roll her eyes when I'd say; 'Sorry Mich, that guy's got a granddad with him who wants to say hello!'

She used to comment that it was *very* suspicious it was always the good-looking ones who had the dead relatives in

tow – never the nerds! (It was coincidence, Mich, honest!)
I'd march purposely over to the guy in question and half startle them to death with my highly original chat-up line; 'Hi there, I'm Anne. Your granddad would like a quick natter with you!' I always ended up huddled in a corner of the club with someone or other. To the casual observer, it must've looked like we were getting quite intense and cosy. If only they'd known the truth!

Away from the hazy, alcohol-induced, dimmed lights of the nightclub world, there was no way on God's Green Earth that I would've had the guts to approach anyone. I was an extremely shy, nervous type of person. But without those early reads I don't think I would've ever had the confidence to read professionally. They definitely played an important part in my spiritual development, and I'm pleased I managed to reach many people (well, men) that would never in a billion years have gone to see a medium. All I can say is, thank God for Bacardi and Coke!

Back from our holiday and all fired up from the reading I'd given in the club, I decided that it might be a good idea to try out some sort of spiritual activity. I was now attending the church every so often, and I saw a leaflet on the notice board advertising a meditation circle. I didn't really have a clue what meditation was, but it sounded good, so I thought I'd give it a shot.

Ah, meditation! That wonderful state that is soooo easy to achieve! Where the body is relaxed and your mind is free to wander off into the Higher Realms. Where anything can happen... from being whisked off into The Light by shining beings of infinite wisdom, who'll hand you the keys to inner peace and happiness... to being shown the most amazing scenes on the mirror of your subconscious mind...
Yeah, right!

Meditation is a very personal thing, and I'm sure many people have experienced the above, but for me, meditation is a very subtle thing, and can be quite tricky to master – as I was just about to discover!

The evening of the meditation group arrived and nervously I took my seat, hardly able to contain my excitement. I wasn't quite sure what I was expecting, but at the very least, I thought I would meet some amazing beings from 'The Spirit World'!

About eight of us sat in a circle, and the tutor told us to relax and close our eyes. Five minutes later the room was filled with deep even breathing and the soothing sounds of the ocean, courtesy of the tape recorder. I opened one eye a slither to peek at the others. They all seemed to be in a calm relaxed state, apart from the tutor who was observing us. He caught my slithered eye and frowned. Quickly I shut it and tried hard to focus...

'You are strolling along a beautiful beach. You can feel the water lapping gently at your feet. Someone is coming along to greet you. Yes, there they are! Notice what they are wearing, how they look. This is your Guide. They are telling you something. Something important! Something wonderful! What is it?'

I was starting to panic. I couldn't see any beach. Not even a grain of sand! For some unexplained reason Fred Flintstone kept popping into my mind. Flipping fantastic! *Fred Flintstone is my Guide*! What is Fred telling me? Could this be symbolic? I asked myself. Hmm. Or could it be to do with the fact I'd watched a *Flintstone* cartoon the previous day?

Then the inevitable bit; one by one we had to 'share' our experience with the group.

Help, Fred! Anyone? Help!

'Shall we start with you?' the tutor asked a lady called Sally. Sally was breathing heavily and dabbing her eyes with a tissue.

'Take your time, Sally,' the tutor advised gently.

'It was just the most incredible experience,' Sally began enthusiastically. 'I was taken to this beautiful Greek temple, with pillars and everything.'

Temple! It was supposed to be a beach! I thought grudgingly.

'I met this kind elderly gentleman dressed in a pure white robe, who told me I had a special purpose to fulfil on earth. He promised he would be there always to help me.'

The tutor beamed at Sally. 'That's wonderful!'

Oh, God! She gets all that and I get Fred Flintstone! Life is indeed unfair.

This carried on much the same. One guy had had a natter with Buddha, an elderly lady a meeting with a disguised monk.

Then it got to me.

So what did I do? Fib, of course!

Everyone sat open-mouthed as I relayed my encounter to the Higher Realms, and my meeting with the Archangel Gabrielle.

One thing I'll never forget is the look on the tutor's face as I muttered my way through my incredible inner-journey.

Oh yes, the tutor knew all right that I wasn't being completely honest. And I'm not proud of fibbing, but what could I do? Tell them I had a cartoon caveman for a guide?

For quite a few years after this early experience I had the same problem with meditation. I got a bit tired of having to sit and listen to other people's 'wonderful spiritual adventures' while I got a big fat nothing. It wasn't until I started reading professionally that I was finally able to appreciate meditation. Oh, well, as they say better late than never – and at least Fred never made a re-appearance. I guess he wasn't my guide after all!

It was just a few months after this meditation class that I met my first serious boyfriend, Robert. 'The Robert Years' felt like what I imagine being inside a washing machine feels like – very turbulent! Robert wasn't a bad guy, but he *was* extremely emotional. I was never quite sure what mood he was going to be in from one moment to the next. He could be so loving and gentle, then like a flash he'd turn on me in a very aggressive manner. These were dark days for me, but Robert and I *did* have some good times together.

It was while I was living with Robert at his parents' house in Walton-on-Thames that I started 'seeing things'. (And no, I wasn't back on the Bacardi and Coke!)

Let me explain. When I'm giving a reading, I 'see' people and objects in my mind's eye, but since I was eighteen I've also seen people and objects with my normal eyes. This only happens when I'm in a very relaxed state, but I'm not asleep. Over the past twenty years, I've seen countless objects and people, and some of these have had very significant meaning, as you will see. I'm still trying to figure out the true meaning behind some of these visions, and I will explore this further in another chapter.

The very first thing I recall seeing physically was a green-and-white-striped shirt, neatly folded and sitting on the arm of our sofa bed.

The room was full of early morning light as I lay there, staring at this shirt. I remember wondering how it'd suddenly just appeared out of nowhere overnight. It certainly didn't look like a shirt Robert would wear. Whilst I was staring at it, it started to dissolve, within seconds fading away to nothing.

What on earth...

I started to shake Robert awake, yelling at him about what I'd just witnessed.

Robert pushed my arms away. 'Go back to sleep,' he murmured. 'You're dreaming, you silly moo.'

I didn't know what to make of it, but I knew that I *definitely* hadn't been dreaming.

Interestingly, the only other time I saw a shirt like that

was three years later… on the first date with my future husband, Andy!

Robert's best mate, Paul, was a fantastic guy; witty, kind, hard-working, and also great fun. Paul always brought out the best in Robert. He had a very calming effect on my highly-strung boyfriend.

Some of the best times I had with Robert were when Paul was about. Paul was a very deep, sensitive soul, and we often used to discuss philosophical subjects like religion and what happened when you, in his words, 'snuffed it'!

One evening, a couple of years later, when Robert and I were no longer an item, I was in bed, reading. I glanced up and standing there, blankly staring at me, was this silent tall figure dressed in a black hooded robe. The only way to describe this creature's sudden appearance is terrifying. I was too scared to scream, or even move.

To my utter relief, a few moments later the figure faded. But I was left shaking with fear, and drowning in this hideous feeling of doom.

The next day I had a call from Robert. He was in bits. Paul had hanged himself. I was shocked. As I tried to console Robert, all I could think of was the fearsome apparition I'd experienced. Had it been some sort of warning of the bad news to come? It had to be! Because of this disturbing vision I was extremely concerned that it meant Paul might be floating around in the ether his poor Soul not 'at rest'.

I asked Spirit to tell me if he'd crossed over okay. I'd read that people who take their own lives could have problems passing over to Spirit; although I now know that this is *extremely* rare.

A week or so later I got my answer. I saw Paul. Only his head and shoulders, but there he was cheekily grinning down at me. His lips were moving, but I don't know what he was trying to say. Then he faded.

I couldn't thank the spirit people enough. From the moment I'd seen Paul's familiar grin, I just knew he was totally fine.

On the 13th November 1989, three days before my twenty-first birthday, I experienced the worst day of my life. Nan passed over.

Although I'd lost Granddad the previous year it was Nan's death that really affected me. She was in her eighties, so it was hardly unexpected, but I'd lived with her all my life, and she was my very best friend. I was utterly devastated.

Two days before Nan had passed over she told us she'd seen Granddad sitting in his usual chair, gazing at her. She commented that the miserable old git was actually *smiling*! Everyone thought she must've been going a bit doolally, but I'm absolutely convinced Granddad had come to 'collect' his beloved Malvina.

A few weeks after Nan's passing I was desperate to get some sort of contact with her, so I booked in to see a medium called Mrs Davies. All that week I nagged Nan to make an appearance. I also begged her for a specific piece of evidence – to mention a ring Mum had given me that had been Nan's favourite possession.

On the morning of the reading I was a complete bundle of nerves. Dragging along the ever suffering Michelle, we managed to get lost as we drove to the medium's house near Staines. We turned up about two hours late, and it was obvious that Mrs Davies wasn't too happy. I don't blame her! She was very nice about it though, and said she'd still read for both of us.

She led us into her very cosy 'reading' room. Michelle had her reading first. All I can remember is that a black kitten came through for her, which surprised me, as Michelle is not what you would call an animal lover. Mich kept insisting that she didn't understand anything about a kitten, so Mrs Davies, looking frustrated, turned her attention to me.

After a few minutes, Mrs Davies linked with Nan. In fairness I can't remember the details of the reading. I'm sure they were good, but all I kept thinking was; *Nan, mention the ring. Mention I've got your ring.*

That was the *only* piece of evidence I would accept. I realise now that I probably missed out on a lot of good evidence and messages because I was so totally obsessed with that one thing.

Half-hour later and *still* there was no mention of the key piece of evidence. Feeling deflated, and wondering if the whole thing *was* a load of hocus-pocus after all, we stood up to leave. Silently, I pleaded once more; *Please Nan, if you're okay mention the ring!*

Mrs Davies suddenly grabbed my hand. 'Oh, wait a second. Your grandmother just said that you've got her ring. Look after it, won't you, dear?'

Yes!!! Nan had come up trumps for me – and Mrs Davies, of course!

She hadn't described the ring, but that didn't matter. I now know that rings aren't what you'd call fantastic evidence, as they're quite common, but I know that in *my* case Nan knew I really needed to hear this particular piece of evidence.

After my reading I felt so much relief. With that one line Mrs Davies helped so much. I still missed Nan like crazy, but now I felt I was able to cope with her passing.

Nan has visited me numerous times over the years, and *twice* I've physically seen her, but I'll come to that later...

Interestingly, I was giving a reading to a lady in Woking last year, when I linked with an elderly lady in Spirit who told me her name was Mrs Davies. There was a tremendously strong spiritual feeling radiating from this spirit lady. The woman I was reading for explained she'd been sitting in a development circle ran by a Mrs Davies – but she had just passed over. After a few more details had been revealed, it was obvious that this was *the same* Mrs Davies who had read for me twenty years previously. I could hardly believe it!

Oh yes, and before I forget. If you were wondering about Michelle's reading and the mysterious black kitten, she admitted on the way home that at aged five she'd accidentally trapped the family kitten in a drawer, and it'd passed away. She'd always felt guilty about it. The kitten had come through to let her know he was fine.

2

Hello, Andy! Goodbye, Dad!

My life changed when I met Andy. Andy wasn't really in to spiritual things when I met him. The only interest he had in the paranormal was a vague interest in UFOs. He would patiently listen to my frequent ramblings on my various spiritual beliefs, or raving on about the latest esoteric book I'd read.

One evening Andy and I were driving home from a meal celebrating my birthday. Our route back to Andy's flat in Addlestone took us past Windsor Castle. I absolutely adore castles, so I feasted my eyes upon it, blissfully taking in the beauty radiating from that wonderful old building.

Back home in bed, I couldn't sleep. There was this strange ringing noise, like someone clanging a bell in my ears, mostly my right ear to be more precise. I could also make out one word constantly repeating... *Fire! Fire! Fire*!

It was extremely disconcerting. After a couple of hours I managed to fall asleep, and by the morning it seemed to have stopped, so I put it down to being over-tired and forgot about it.

But that night the clanging started up again. This time it was even louder than the previous night. Then the shouting started; *Fire! Fire! Fire!* At one point it was so loud I got out of bed and stuck my head out of the window to see if it could be coming from outside. But no, it wasn't.

After the third night I was seriously beginning to worry that I might be losing the plot. I'd experienced Spirit voices before, but only as information that 'popped' into my head and was gone – not this constant drone of just one repeating word.

In desperation, I asked Spirit what was going on. Immediately I had the strong impression of an old building, which I thought was a cathedral. I could 'see' huge billows of smoke pouring from the building. Seconds later the vivid image faded.

Sitting in Andy's flat, my stomach was in huge knots as I told Andy about my weird experience. I expected him to laugh at me, but he didn't.

'What do you think it means?' he enquired, frowning slightly.

'I think there's going to be a disaster of some kind,' I told him, studying his face to see his reaction. 'It's connected with a church or cathedral.'

Andy didn't say much. He just stared solemnly at me out of those huge serious eyes of his. Our relationship was fairly newish at this stage, and I wondered if I'd gone and spectacularly blown it by confiding in him with my 'Crazy Stuff'. He was even more quiet than usual as he drove me back home.

I couldn't help thinking; *Oh God, me and my bloody big mouth! I'm carrying sticky-tape around with me from now on!*

The next day Andy called me from his office in Staines.

'You're not going to believe this,' he breathed down the line. 'I was driving over to Slough at lunch, and I could see a load of smoke pouring out of Windsor Castle. This is what you were on about, wasn't it? This is your premonition!'

'Yes, it must be,' I croaked, feeling pretty stunned.

'How did you do it?'

'I'm not sure,' I replied truthfully. 'I think I must've picked it up when we drove past the castle on my birthday.'

'But how?' he demanded.

Although I was shocked, I couldn't resist smiling to myself. I could almost hear Andy's logical brain whirling away, trying to make sense of the impossible.

'You told me you thought it was a church or cathedral though, so you weren't quite right,' he reminded me smugly.

That was true, but we found out later that the fire had started in the chapel, and I know the impression I got was of a very old stately building. I suppose all this could've been coincidence, but I don't think so.

I'm not sure why I picked up on this particular event. I can only assume it's because – as I'd told Andy – we'd driven by the castle a few days before the fire and I'd somehow tuned in to this future event. Spirit must've decided to use that opportunity to draw me into the world of the '*Twilight Zone*', presumably to trigger off my interest again.

Which it certainly did! I spent the next two years reading as many spiritual books I could get my hands on.

In July 1993 Mum, Dad and I moved from Walton-on-Thames to Guildford in Surrey. Dad was extremely excited and kept stopping to do little comical jigs as we packed endless boxes. For years it'd been his absolute dream to live in this particular road in Guildford, and now it was finally happening.

Whilst Nan and Granddad were alive, it hadn't really been possible, as they'd been too frail to take all the upheaval of moving. Little did we know 'Dad's Dream' was just about to turn into a very real and terrible *nightmare*!

Just a month after we'd moved in, Dad was diagnosed with terminal cancer and was given only a few months to live. He was sixty-two.

Although we knew Dad was dying, it was never openly discussed. We all acted as if he had a bit of a bug and would soon be 'up and about' as usual. I think this was the only way for us all to cope. Dad allowed this charade to take place to protect us from the horror of what was occurring.

I'll never forget the day I was sitting with Dad, rubbing and patting his back to try and relieve the terrible indigestion he was suffering.

'Anne, please don't hold it against me if I kick the bucket,' he suddenly whispered. 'And please don't forget me, will you?'

'Of course not, Dad,' I muttered, feeling my heart shattering into a million bits.

That night I lay tossing and turning in bed. A rage like I'd never felt before was pulsating through me. Dad had had a particularly bad day and I was feeling extremely upset about watching my quiet proud dad go through this terrible disease. I began to rant and rave at Spirit, yelling at them to explain what kind of God would let this terrible thing happen.

When I'd ranted myself silly, I literally begged Spirit that if Dad had to die then at least could they tell me when it would happen, so I could be there for him at the end.

Within minutes tiny particles of coloured lights were appearing above me. They arranged themselves into a distinct image; two cherubs, complete with their Cupid's bow and arrow.

This image was not in my mind, nor was it a fleeting image in the dark. It was shockingly clear and in full colour. I would swear this on a stack of bibles, and I was most definitely *awake*. The cherubs didn't have the quality of being real; they were more like a still image you might see in a book. The image was there for around ten or so seconds, then faded. I had seen things before – such as the horrifying apparition the night Paul had died – but this was so obviously in response to my earlier chat to Spirit.

What did it mean though? I couldn't understand how cherubs related to Dad passing away.

A few weeks later I got my answer. I was watching something on telly when a cherub appeared on the screen advertising some programme for Valentine's Day, which was the following week. It was then the penny dropped so to speak. They were telling me that Valentine's Day was the day Dad would pass over. I suppose thinking about it, if it had been any other day I'm not sure how they would've explained it to me, but I'm sure they would've found a way.

I only told Mum about my 'vision', and we both made sure we were around all that day. I spent the day hovering constantly by Dad's bedside. At nine that evening Dad was still sleeping peacefully, pumped with pain-relieving drugs.

I began to doubt Spirit's 'cherub prediction'. I'd popped up to my room at just gone nine, when a voice hissed urgently in my head '*NOW*!' I didn't argue – just bolted downstairs to Dad's makeshift bedroom.

Mum had gone to make a cup of tea for my Aunt Flanders and Uncle Norman, who were there lending their support. I rushed to Dad's bedside and took his hand. Within a minute he took his last breath. I whispered I loved him and told him to go towards the light.

A sense of peace and calm rippled through me. I sensed Spirit people in the room, but I was only 25 and wasn't a working medium at this point, so couldn't really say who it was. (I know now that the people I sensed had been Dad's mother and father – which I suppose is logical.)

Uncle Norman popped his head round the door.

'He's gone,' I said quietly, still clutching Dad's hand.

'Poor Fred,' muttered Uncle Nor.

Mum came in. Silently she stared down at the man she'd been married to for nearly forty years, then left to make the necessary calls.

The next couple of hours are a bit of a blur, but there is one thing I clearly remember. It occurred shortly after Dad's passing. We were all sitting in the front room having a cup of tea, when the wall-lights flashed very definitely three times. I'd never seen them flash like that before, and they never did again. I'm sure it was Dad saying his goodbyes.

I did tell quite a few people about my 'cherub experience', but could tell by their reaction that they thought my pain and distress at losing Dad had manifested the image of the cherubs. I'm sure that's what most psychologists would insist had happened, but I *know* that what I saw was Spirit's way of telling me Dad's passing date, so that I could be there for him. I will be eternally grateful to my unseen friends for giving me that information, and I like to think that the words I whispered to Dad helped him on his way.

A few months after Dad's passing I was sitting in my bedroom feeling incredibly dejected. I didn't have a 'proper' job as such, but had been trying to write children's books.

So far, although I'd had some very positive comments, everything I'd submitted had been politely declined.

I did the odd day's work at a centre for the elderly, but that was something I didn't really want to do full-time. By this time Andy had sold his flat in Addlestone and had moved in with Mum and me. If he hadn't done this, we probably would've had to sell Dad's Dream House, as there was no way Mum and I could've afforded its upkeep.

I was reading a lot of Stephen O'Brien's fascinating books around this time. What an incredible inspiration this man was to me at this point in my life!

Apart from Doris Stokes I think Stephen was the first celebrity medium. One day, after reading a particularly moving chapter, I put down the book and literally *begged* Spirit that I might be privileged enough to work alongside them, helping people to understand that death isn't really The End.

Out shopping that afternoon, I bumped into an old school mate called Mark. I hadn't seen Mark for years, and it was great to see him, as we were quite good mates at school. We got chatting, and he mentioned that he was sitting in a development circle. I was surprised, as I never knew he was interested in any sort of psychic stuff. I kind of knew what a development circle was, but I'd never sat in one myself. I told him about the request I'd made that very morning of my desire to work for Spirit. Mark immediately said he'd ask his circle if they'd let me sit with them one evening.

How Spirit organises these types of meetings for us, with certain people at certain times, is totally beyond me, but to do it *that* fast was a bit mind-blowing!

'You Lot, I'm impressed!' I muttered as I raced home to tell Andy.

The following week, Mark kindly picked me up from Guildford. I was shaking from nerves, not really knowing what to expect. What if they wanted me to stand up and get someone through? I would end up looking like a complete and utter idiot in front of everyone.

On the way there, I kept up a polite flow of conversation, trying to give the impression of confidence, but I just wanted to go home and watch *Coronation Street,* and have a nice cup of tea and a custard slice with Mum and Andy.

We soon arrived at a neat looking bungalow belonging to the couple running the circle.

'Are you okay?' Mark asked as he parked the car. 'You look a bit nervous.'

I nodded. 'I'm fine.'

'They're fantastic people, so don't worry. They won't bite. Honest.'

Mark was right. Inside I was immediately embraced by June, the lady of the house.

'Hello, Anne. Thanks for joining us this evening. It's really lovely to meet you.'

I smiled. 'Thanks very much for inviting me.'

Looking around I realised that half the people looked vaguely familiar. I'd seen four of five of them before, down Walton Spiritualist church. I wasn't sure it they recognised me though.

In total about ten of us squeezed snugly into June's lounge. Her husband surprised me by offering me a vodka and tonic. He must've picked up on my boozy past! The reason this shocked me was because I'd read that it wasn't advisable to drink any alcohol before attempting any sort of psychic work. I took it, but left it under my chair.

While June opened the circle with a short prayer, I slipped my hand into my pocket and clutched Nan's ring as if my life depended on it.

'Do you mind if we use you to practice on, Anne?' June enquired, after she'd finished the prayer.

'Of course not, that'd be fantastic,' I beamed, my heart leaping with pure relief. What? They didn't want me to do anything? I could just sit back and enjoy being 'read for' by nine budding mediums. Yesss! This was like a dream come true.

'Of course you'll have your chance to work a bit later, if you'd like,' June said, smiling encouragingly at me. 'After all, we're all here to develop, aren't we?'

'Thanks,' I croaked, feeling the heat flaring up on my face and neck. For God's sake, what was wrong with me? This was ridiculous! Of course I'd come here to work. I should be jumping up and down with excitement at the opportunity – but all I felt was an intense fear of failure.

Everyone else seemed keen to get going, so in turn they each gave me a mini-reading. A couple of them linked with Nan and Granddad, but mostly it was psychic based titbits about my life. I can't recall most of it, but one very sweet elderly lady told me she could see me writing children's stories with pictures. I thought this was good as I *was* writing children's stories, which none of them knew. The picture bit puzzled me, as I was writing for older children, but later this premonition turned out to be spot on.

The last one to give me a reading was the group leader, June.

I thought she wasn't picking up anything at first, because she was quiet for so long. She sat with her head perched at an angle as if listening to a silent voice, which I suppose she was. Finally, she began to speak, very slowly and precisely;

'My guide is telling me they have plans for you, young lady. They have heard your request and want to assure you that you will most *definitely* be working as a medium in the near future. They're saying the only limits you'll *ever* have are those you impose on yourself. Your journey won't be an easy one, but you'll never be alone. Your link with Spirit will be incredibly strong. You'll be privileged enough to help many people on both sides of life. Your grandmother will be helping you. Please, please trust in them, Anne.'

I sat open mouthed, feeling my face turning beetroot red.

Was this for real? Was this elderly lady, who radiated such warmth and genuine kindness, having me on? Pandering to my ego with a few chosen words that any young person would be delighted to hear? I glanced over at Mark. He looked pretty stunned, as did the rest of the group.

June bent down and took a sip of her water. I must admit, I did wonder if her 'water' might really be vodka after hearing her reading to me!

'Right. Yes, err, okay, thanks...' I stammered weakly. 'I'll look forward to that!'

June nodded earnestly, 'You mark my words.'

Then came the moment I'd been dreading! 'Do you want to see if you have anything for any of us now, Anne?'

Oh, God! After June's comments, they were probably all going to expect me to be flipping amazing. I'd only ever given a few spontaneous messages in darkened nightclubs whilst I'd been quite tipsy. This was a *completely* different crystal-ball game!

June must've seen the look of horror on my face, as she kindly gave me a 'get out of jail free' card. 'If you want to leave it until next time, that's fine.'

I wish I could report here that I boomed out confidently, 'No. June! I'll give it a shot!' Then tell you I stood up and commenced to give some incredible survival evidence, knocking everyone socks (and shoes) off. Sorry, but I can't.

Yes, I chickened out – Big Time! That very good friend of mine *fear* kicked in, and I muttered that next week would be fine, as I was feeling a little tired.

On the way home, Mark kept glancing over at me.

'What's up?' I asked at last, starting to feel a bit paranoid.

'I've sat in circle with June for three years, and I've *never* heard her talk like that about anyone. It's just not her way. She's rarely ever wrong with her predictions.'

There's always a first time! I thought negatively. I was flattered, but didn't really believe any of her words to me.

Looking back, I can't believe how little faith I had in myself, or in Spirit.

A few days later Mark rang me to tell me that I'd been officially invited to attend the circle on a regular basis. Apparently, I was the first person in two years to be offered this privilege. No wonder they needed to practise on me!

I thought about it, but declined, after deciding that I didn't want to put Mark out every week, as he'd kindly offered to pick me up.

It took a while for me to admit to myself the *real* reason I'd turned down the offer. Ironically, June's reading had put me off. I couldn't stand the thought of letting her down by being rubbish.

Fear has a lot to answer for!

This one isolated evening was, and still is, my only experience of sitting in a mental mediumship development circle. I did almost all my training the hard way – on my own...

3

My First Readings!

On March 16th 1996, I got hitched to Andy at Walton Spiritualist church.

The very church Michelle and I had gone to (and nearly got kicked out of) all those years earlier. In fact, our registrar was the same lady who'd frowned down at us from the platform as we'd attempted to control our giggles!

As I stepped into my beautiful fairy-tale wedding dress, I felt a lump form in my throat. Dad *should* be here walking me down the aisle. Instead, my Uncle Norman was 'giving me away'.

A few moments before the cars arrived to take us to the church, I found myself standing on my own in the hallway of Dad's Dream House.

'Dad, please be at my wedding,' I whispered. For a split second I had a very strong sense of someone standing behind me. I whirled round, but no one was there. Had it been Dad? To this day, I couldn't say for certain.

When I first started to read professionally, it surprised me how many spirit people mentioned events, important and insignificant, occurring in their loved ones' lives. They seemed to be very much aware of what was going on in our world. I assumed they'd visit us occasionally, but the longer I've been a medium I've come to the conclusion that they're around *much* more than we'd ever realise. Of course, they enjoy their new spiritual surroundings, but they're still very interested in our day-to-day lives. It's only natural that they want to see what's going on, be kept in the loop, so to speak. I know if I was over there I would still pop down and have a nose about to see what my family and mates were up to! Wouldn't you?

After all the excitement of the wedding had faded and we'd returned from our Lake District honeymoon, life seemed pretty flat. Andy had been made redundant the day before we'd got married. Great timing to start a new life! The only bright spot was that he'd received quite a decent redundancy payment. He decided to use it to set up his own computer consultancy business.

It was at this time that I had a breakthrough with my children's writing. I wrote a short story and sent it to *Mandy,* a picture-story publication for girls. They bought it for their Annual. I don't think I've ever felt so happy in my entire life. Better still, they asked me if I would be interested in writing scripts for their weekly publications *Mandy* and *Bunty*.

It was a real dream come true for me, because as a young girl I'd adored these magazines, and couldn't have asked for a better job! For the next year, I wrote quite a few scripts, which were sent off to an artist who would bring my stories to life on paper.

The lady from the development circle I'd attended with Mark had been bang on with her prediction of me writing with pictures! Unfortunately, I never saw her again to tell her how accurate she'd been!

On the spiritual front this was a very quiet time for me. I was still having regular visions of various people and objects, but I wasn't actively trying to develop my psychic abilities. Occasionally, June's words about my spiritual future drifted into my mind, but I just shrugged them off, telling myself she'd been mistaken with that particular prediction.

I was devastated when one day I received a letter informing me that *Mandy* was folding. It seemed that young girls were no longer interested in picture-stories. I'd seen myself writing for them for years to come, and had literally hundreds of plot ideas scribbled down for future development. Now what was I going to do? Andy had been trying his best with his computer business, but unfortunately it just wasn't taking off. We discussed him getting a conventional job, but he admitted that he'd really lost his confidence when he'd been made redundant and couldn't face getting a nine to five job just yet.

The *Mandy* letter in my hand, I lay on the bed feeling scared to death about the future. Andy had sold his flat in Addlestone at a rock bottom price. Now, properties were booming again, and there was no way we could afford to get back on the ladder. Mum and Andy weren't getting on at all, they argued almost continually. I felt like piggy-in-the-middle, always trying to keep the peace between them. Depression overwhelmed me at the prospect of having to live with Mum for the rest of our lives. As much as I loved her it just wasn't working, but there really didn't seem to be any way round it.

'Spirit, can you please help us?' I whispered into the darkness.

I didn't hear a reply. We were on our own... or so I thought!

A week later, I received an unexpected phone call that set off a chain of events that changed our lives forever!

The phone call was from Diane, my brother Rick's ex-wife.

I was really surprised to hear her warm northern accent down the line, as I hadn't spoken to Diane for ages. She and Rick had been divorced for a few years by now, and Diane had gone back to live in Lancashire, where she'd re-married a man called Mick.

'How are you?' I enquired awkwardly. I've never been that fluid with phone conversations.

'I'm extremely well,' Diane replied happily. Diane had suffered from a lot of health problems throughout her life, and had completely lost her sight at 28 because of complications with her diabetes. She'd also had a kidney transplant, so she'd definitely not had an easy few years. It was great to hear her sounding so chirpy. We chatted about our families for a while, catching up on all the news. I also confided in her about the financial stress we were going through with our work situations.

'We might just have the solution for you!' Diane blurted excitedly. 'This is why I'm calling, actually. Mick and I have started a network marketing business selling aloe vera health products. That's why I'm so well at the moment. The products are truly amazing.'

'Right,' I said slowly, wondering where this was going. Her warm tone of voice suddenly turned sharp and professional as she proceeded to give me a twenty minute lecture on the benefits of network marketing. I never even *heard* of network marketing.

In the end I asked her to send me some information about the business opportunity. She made it sound so fantastic and easy, but being a very sceptical person I had my doubts about the sort of income that was supposedly possible within a few months.

I told Andy about the call, and he straight off said he wasn't the slightest bit interested. Always the voice of reason he pointed out that we had no sales experience, and what was this aloe vera, anyway? Was it someone's elderly aunt? Ha, ha, very funny, Andy!

I shrugged it off, and when, a few days later, the literature popped through the post, it went straight in the bin. So that was the end of that – or so I thought. But I didn't take Diane's persistence into account!

After a few more phone calls, we reluctantly agreed to attend a meeting in Birmingham to hear all about this miracle aloe vera drink. In all honestly I only agreed to go because I wanted to see Diane again. As a child I'd been extremely fond of her, and vividly remembered the amazing spiritual conversations I'd had with her and Rick.

The meeting is a bit of a blur. All I remember is loads of very smartly dressed people going on stage and boasting about how much money they were earning just by sponsoring five people to do the business, and them doing the same, and so on and so on...

The long and short of it was; we decided to give it a go. All we needed was a box of products, which cost about two hundred pounds, and we were off.

The other deciding factor for me was Diane's amazing appearance. Now in her forties, she looked better than ever. She swore to me that also she'd never *felt* so good since using the aloe products. I must admit I was eager and excited to try out for myself the array of creams and lotions the company sold, and by joining we got the products at wholesale price.

Someone at the meeting had suggested a good place to sell the products was at craft fairs, but scanning the local newspaper I couldn't spot any that we could call. I *did* notice a small advert for a psychic fair at Guildford Civic Hall, so we decided to pop along and have a talk with the organiser.

Once at the fair, I left Andy to chat to a very pleasant young guy with long sandy hair in a ponytail. I thought that as I was there I might as well have a reading. Deciding whom to pick out of the eight or so readers was a task in itself. I really needed guidance, and wondered if Dad or Nan would help. Thirty pounds was a lot of money to waste if I chose the wrong reader! In the end I opted for an attractive youngish lady with long dark hair and a gentle caring face. I think her name was Fran. She was working with a battered pack of tarot cards. However, she assured me that they were only a tool, and she could also link with The Spirit World!

True to her word, before I'd even finished shuffling the pack she'd linked with an ex-boyfriend of mine who'd been killed in a car accident. His name had been Bert, short for Herbert, which he absolutely detested! I can't blame him on that one – apologies to any Herberts out there reading this! I went out with him for about three months when I was sixteen, so it was hardly the Romance of the Century! Bert was what you would call a rough diamond. I knew he was a bit of a Bad Boy, a Troublemaker, but he'd always been really kind and loving in our short time together. All the same, I couldn't understand why he was stepping forward for me. Where was Dad or Nan, or even Grumpy Granddad?

'What does *he* want?' I blurted out quite rudely.

'He just wants you to know he saw your wedding, and is very pleased you're happy. He says he'll keep an eye on you from time to time.'

Hmm! Not sure I liked the sound of that! Hope he wasn't watching too closely! I smiled politely and asked her to thank him.

Whilst I'd been dating Bert I'd had a very intense dream, which to this day I vividly remember;

Bert and I were in a car, driving down a quiet country road. There were fields looking out on my side, and trees on his. The music was blaring out and we were laughing about something. Then Bert had suddenly lost control of the car and had hit a tree. I'd abruptly woken up; incredibly relieved it'd been just a horrible nightmare.

But it had left such a strong impression on me I really didn't like getting in a car with him from then on (although I did a couple of times). It was a couple of years or so after the dream that I heard the terrible news about Bert's accident.

I'm not sure if this dream was meant as some kind of warning for me. I've always felt a little guilty, as I never mentioned the dream to Bert. I knew he'd laugh his head off if I'd said anything. I suppose the dream could've come from my sub-conscious, as Bert wasn't the most careful driver in the world!

Apart from Bert making an appearance in my reading, a few other things were said involving my own psychic abilities, which I can't remember in any detail. I *do* remember healing was mentioned, something that I wasn't particularly drawn to. Then Fran asked me if I had any questions.

I nodded. 'My husband and I are starting a new business and I was wondering if you got any feelings about it?'

Up until this point there hadn't been any concrete evidence in the reading. True, she'd picked up a 'young lad' who'd died in an accident, which I'd taken to be Bert, but nothing *really* specific. Ever the sceptic, I'm always looking for information that could *not* be guessed or got in any other way except through the psychic channels. But Fran really surprised me with her next comment.

'Is this business connected to complimentary therapies of some kind?' she asked, as she stared intently at the cards I'd picked out.

'Yes, it is,' I said, quietly impressed.

Fran's eyebrows were almost touching because she was frowning so much as she continued studying the cards. My stomach flipped a little as I watched her expression.

'In all honesty I don't get a great feeling about this business,' she said bluntly. 'It's going to take up a lot of your time, energy and finances, but I don't believe you're going to do very well with it.'

I was shaken up, taken aback with her brutal honestly. 'Are you sure?'

Fran nodded. 'Maybe you could do it as a hobby,' she suggested gently.

We'd just spent two hundred quid on a box of products to start a business, and this lady was telling me to treat it as a hobby! I know it doesn't sound like a massive sum of money, but to us it was.

I told Andy about the reading, but he shrugged it off, and we decided to go ahead anyway. As Andy said, you couldn't base a decision like that on the say of a psychic, could you...?

He told me that the fair organiser, Adrian, had said he'd be happy for us to hire a table off him for our products. He would charge us a small fee for the privilege, but that was expected.

We purchased a dark-green crushed velvet cloth, to cover the table, and apprehensively set off for our first psychic fair at Woking leisure centre.

And so a new era in our lives started. Three evenings a week, and most weekends, we travelled to fairs, sometimes quite a distance, setting up our aloe vera stall, and trying to convince people that these products would enhance their lives immensely.

It was extremely hard work, and most of the time we barely made enough to pay our table-rent, let alone petrol and other expenses. But despite all this, I thoroughly enjoyed the spiritual environment.

I absolutely adored getting all the gossip from a member of the public about their reading. Finding out about how fantastic (or rubbish) it'd been, when really I should've been concentrating on selling them a tube of aloe toothpaste, or a moisturiser.

At each fair, I drove Andy round the twist by disappearing quicker than an extra-large bar of fruit and nut at a chocoholics' convention! I would spend the evenings drifting round the hall or hotel, my eyes feasting on the goodie-laden crystal stall, or flicking through the spiritual books and CDs on sale. The readers always seemed like mysterious, magical people to me, and I was so in awe I hardly spoke to them. As we were running a stall that wasn't spiritual in any way, I always felt like I was on the outside looking in on a world I so much wanted to be part of, but couldn't. The best I could hope for was to hear the excitement and happiness of a member of the public who'd had a great reading.

I used to fantasies that one of the readers would one day rush over to me and comment on my amazing aura, or tell me they were picking up what a brilliant medium I would make, but no such luck. I obviously wasn't registering on the psychic radar. It was tough being surrounded by people that were living out my own personal dream, doing what I truly wanted to do, and not believing for a second that I would ever have enough confidence in my abilities to be able to 'do it'.

We'd been with the fairs for around eighteen months when once again we received an unexpected phone call. It turned out to be this call that finally helped me to turn my dream of being a medium into a reality.

The call was from a guy called Pete. He was starting up some holistic fairs and had somehow got hold of one of our aloe leaflets. He asked us if we wanted to do some fairs with him.

As the venues he was doing were closer to home, and he was charging us less for the table, we agreed.

My guides have admitted to me that they orchestrated the whole psychic fair thing. The aloe business was used as a way to ease me into that spiritual environment. When things hadn't happened for me at Adrian's fairs, they'd had Pete step in. One way or another they were quite determined for me to work with them, and it worked – in the end!

Interestingly, the reading I'd had with Fran turned out to be spot on. So far, the aloe business *had* proved to be more or less a waste of time and money. Although to be fair my skin was now looking great, and it had cleared up Andy's sore gums, so it hadn't been a complete waste of time! BUT... *what if we'd taken her advice and not done the business*? This is where the future is an *extremely* tricky and complex subject. It was very important that we did the aloe vera – even if it'd failed – so that the sequence of events could unfold as they were meant to.

Pete was probably the most flamboyant, eccentric and forceful person I'd ever met. Going through life, you would probably only ever meet one person like him. If he took a liking to you then he would do absolutely anything for you, but if he didn't...

For some strange reason I was one of the few lucky ones, to start with in any case.

After a few months, we were still struggling with selling anything on the aloe stall. Pete took pity on us and kindly asked if we wanted to go with him to a private psychic party, to try and 'flog some of that disgusting drink' as he put it so eloquently, whilst he was doing the readings.

On the way to the party I plucked up the courage and asked Pete a question that slotted in place the very last piece of my psychic jigsaw.

'Pete, do you run a development circle?'

Pete wrinkled his nose as if he smelled bad drains. 'Why would anyone need a development circle? Like charm, you've either got it or you ain't! Why you asking anyway, sweetie?'

I then proceeded to tell him about the various experiences I'd had, and about the spirit people I was still seeing on a regular basis.

He didn't say very much, in fact he went very quiet – which was most unusual! I felt bitterly disappointed. As Pete was an established medium, I'd been hoping for some sound advice from him.

We arrived at the house in Hemel Hempstead and were made to feel very welcome by Betty, the hostess of the party. She had about six of her friends there, all looking flushed and a little nervous about the evening ahead.

It soon became apparent that our products weren't of any interest to the group, so we packed them up and slung them back in the car. Pete had given each of the ladies a short personal reading. Now he was going to attempt to do some trance-mediumship in front of everyone!

I felt quite excited as I settled down with the others in Betty's cosy lounge. This was my first time at witnessing trance-mediumship. I'd read about it, and had even watched a rather tacky video of some strange bald guy attempting it, but had never seen it first-hand before...

Pete explained that his guide would draw so close to him it would be as if they would actually become one person. He shut his eyes and started to breathe very deeply, his face screwed up in concentration. To my horror, as I watched him I felt the giggles rising inside me. I thought I'd been transported back to being thirteen again (and this time I couldn't even blame the giggles on Michelle).

Everyone else looked suitably serious, so I pulled myself together and swallowed the laughter down as best as I could.

Pete's guide, a Chinese philosopher, started to speak in a very slow, deep monotone.

I can't recall a lot of what was said, but the gist of it was commenting on how humanity should go with the flow in life more often. Water was mentioned several times (which was a little annoying as I was bursting for the loo).

Then the guide went round and gave a little personal message to each person. I waited patiently for him to get round to me, wondering what would be said.

Finally, it was my turn. '*Your hands were not made for washing up, my dear*,' was the first comment the guide made, sticking to the water theme.

I thought it was a bit of a weird thing to say, but nodded, glancing at Andy to see what he thought. He was rolling his eyes. I could hear his brain ticking away, annoyed that I now had a bona fide reason for getting out of dishwashing. Ha!

The guide continued; '*We have plans for you, but first you must take a leap of faith*!'

What followed was eerily familiar to what June had said in her reading to me a few years previously. I must admit, I was a little suspicious. How come this was being mentioned by Pete/China-man, just as we'd had our conversation in the car? I sighed. It wasn't much fun being so flipping sceptical.

When Pete 'returned to his body' he pointed at me and announced loudly, 'You're reading.'

I frowned, puzzled. 'Sorry?'

'You're reading. Now!'

I was starting to feel a little uneasy. 'What do you mean, now?'

Pete grinned. 'I'm throwing you in at the deep end, sweetie. My guide told me it's the only way you'll do it. And after our little chat I know you're ready. I want you to take each of these good people and give them a reading.'

My mouth dropped open. 'What, right now this second?'

'Yep. Right now, this second. Okay?'

The others were very enthusiastic about this idea. 'Go on, Anne. We'll be kind, honest,' the hostess laughed.

Looking round at the eager faces, I knew that I wasn't going to be given a 'get out of jail free' card this time. So I nodded in resignation.

Pete marched me off to a separate tiny room at the back of the house, and instructed me to 'call in my guides'!

I think that at this point calling 999 was more on my mind...

By the time I'd finished my psychic debut it was well past midnight. I was completely knackered, but my very first 'proper' readings had gone exceptionally well. I'm sure that That Lot Upstairs had pushed the psychic boat out, so to speak. After all, if I'd been rubbish I would've been mortified, and doubt that I would've done another reading ever again!

Once I had got over my initial nerves, the information had just flowed through me. It was beautiful. That's the only way I can describe it. The pictures in my mind were crisp and bright, the words sharp and clear. I could tell Betty and the others were really impressed with the readings, and were not just 'being kind'.

On the way back Pete shocked me by telling (not asking) me that I was reading at the next psychic fair.

'You can charge fiver a reading to start with,' he said thoughtfully. 'How does that sound?'

Flipping heck! Doing a few free readings was one thing, but charging... Didn't I need years of training before I could do that?

I started to protest, but Pete cut through me. 'Trust me; you're as ready as you'll ever be, sweetie.'

I glanced in the back seat. Pete had his eyes shut. The subject was closed.

4

Promise To Dad

Two months later, I had seventeen fairs under my belt, and had read for the grand total of 64 people. It was all going incredibly well – apart from one thing. I was suffering terribly with nerves before each fair, and sometimes even the days leading up to a fair. It wasn't getting easier, it was actually getting harder. My stomach felt so churned up before a fair, I couldn't even consider eating! I lost about a stone or so in weight. I weighed just over eight stone at this point, which was the lowest I'd been in over ten years! The only plus point was that people kept asking me what diet I was on, because it was working wonders!

Even now, twelve years on, I still suffer from nerves before a reading, but it's not nearly as intense as in those early days.

I used to tell myself that if I couldn't link the worst that could happen was I would just send them off to see another reader. It was hardly 'End of the World' stuff!

Before each fair I would spend ages in the loo, my stomach churning and gurgling away like a misbehaving washing machine. I was actually sick on a number of occasions. Incredibly, I remember once or twice, when I was particularly suffering with nerves, sitting in the car hoping and praying we'd be involved in a minor accident so we couldn't get there.

I know this all sounds totally ridiculous, but honestly, this is how I felt. Although it was so hard, something *very* powerful drove me on. I just *had* to keep going. While the information I was passing on made sense and was helping people, then there was no way I was giving up. I received many calls from people that I'd read for, thanking me for the experience. In fact, the support I had from them was incredibly moving, and was the reason I *wasn't* going to give in to my old mate Ms Fear.

My first major challenge, reading wise, happened at the Hilton Hotel in Bracknell. It appeared in the shape of a young lady that Pete brought over to my table.

'You've got to read for this lady, Anne,' he hissed urgently at me. 'She needs real spirit communication, not Tarot.'

One look at this young girl's face showed that she was obviously in great emotional distress. Luckily, she had two friends with her, standing either side. Between them they almost had to hold her up!

Pete assured the girl that I would be able to help her, and then breezed off back to man the door.

I really appreciated Pete's faith in my abilities, but in all honesty, I felt completely out of my depth. If I'd had a little more experience I'm not sure I would've attempted to read for her, the state she was in. But with the three of them seated opposite, waiting for me to start, I just did my thing and linked with Spirit.

Immediately, a young man of about twenty stepped forward.

I want to make a strong point here. In writing this book I'm NOT going to 'cherry-pick' the best bits from certain readings. Anyone can pull out their most remarkable survival evidence and look amazing. This book isn't about me trying to prove how wonderful I am. It's about sharing my experiences to hopefully help others expand their understanding and knowledge of the Spiritual Realms. That's why I've only chosen readings that teach us something about Spirit communication.

Going back to the young spirit man; He told me he'd had a motorbike accident, and said the lady was his fiancée.

Her face crumpled as she nodded at my words.

He proceeded to give me a huge amount of specific evidence. The girl's friends had to confirm the information on her behalf, as she just couldn't speak.

In total, I spent about an hour and a half with them, and we were all flipping crying our eyes out by the end of it.

It was obvious he hadn't been over there very long by the sheer raw emotions displayed by the three of them, but I didn't pick up on his passing date.

Finally, they stood up to leave. They all couldn't seem to thank me enough. I'll never forget how awful I felt about taking their thirty pounds, but the two friends insisted, and I did need it to pay my table rent, which was very expensive at that particular venue.

I watched as they left, noticing that the girl didn't need to be supported by her friends any more. She was actually smiling.

I got up to order a cup of tea. I really needed a short break after experiencing all that intense emotion. When I came back in, Pete, sporting a huge beam, called me over. Unexpectedly, he grabbed me and pulled me towards him, embracing me in a bear hug.

'Thank you for doing that, Anne. They were so pleased with what you told them. She's a good friend of mine. Her partner only passed over on Thursday.'

Thursday! But this was Sunday! That meant he'd only died three days ago! No wonder he hadn't mentioned the funeral. They'd not even had it yet!

I'd assumed it was a few months ago or something, but three short days ago! I felt shocked. God, no wonder the poor girl was in such a state.

I think that if I'd known how recently he'd passed over it would've freaked me out, and I might've mentally put up barriers that would've blocked the messages and information that flowed from him so effortlessly.

I'm not quite sure why, but before this reading I had strong ideas that spirit people needed a good few months before attempting to communicate. Now my experience had taught me otherwise.

This reading was my first big lesson – to never stick

Spirit in a box! Over the years there were plenty more lessons in store for me...

One evening, we were at a fair in Cranleigh, a lovely village quite near Guildford, when Pete stomped in the hall, violently shaking a piece of paper he was holding.

Pete circled the tables, showing the contents of the piece of paper to each of us readers in turn. Curiously, I watched each of their faces as they read it and handed it back, but as they each showed completely different emotions, ranging from roars of outrage, indifference, to hoots of laughter, I couldn't hope to guess what the paper said.

Finally, Pete handed it to me.

It was a hand-written letter from a member of the public informing us that what we were doing this evening was '*Evil in the extreme*', and we would '*Pay for it by burning in Hell*'!

Nice!

The writer had also kindly explained that they would be spending the entire evening '*Praying for our Eternal Souls*'.

That was the bit that upset poor Pete. He couldn't stop ranting and raving about '*Not wanting his Eternal 'effing Soul prayed for!*' (Excuse the language.)

I wasn't quite sure *how* to react to the letter. In a strange way I felt quite sorry for the writer. She sounded so desperate and sincere in her concern for our spiritual welfare.

I saw a documentary not so long ago, featuring such a lovely young girl of about twelve. She had such rigid views on religion that it was absolutely heart breaking to see. She obviously suffered such real intense pain for others, and truly believed their fate was sealed (a place reserved in hell) if they so much as told a tiny white lie.

I found tears rolling down my cheeks as I watched her intense little face explaining her beliefs on a God that sounded, to me, so far away from true compassion, wisdom and love! It was obvious that her strong views had been passed on from her highly religious family.

I don't want to get into some sort of heavy religious debate here, as I certainly don't have all (or even a fraction) of the answers. I just believe that any religion or philosophy is a great thing – as long as it helps you feel joyful, and assists you in living YOUR truth. If it brings you or anyone else unhappiness, then maybe that particular 'school of thought' whatever it is, might need to be reconsidered.

My personal belief is that LOVE (not the mushy, flowery type of love) is what's important. Any act that comes from the heart and shows kindness, respect, compassion and understanding of each other, is my definition of Love. Also, embracing and enjoying our differences. That's what counts, in my humble opinion.

Ironically, that night, I actually prayed for the lady who'd written that letter to us '*Devil-Worshipers*' as she'd called us. I prayed that her mind would one day be opened to other endless possibilities and ways to reach God!

I'd been talking to these invisible entities, called 'My Guides' almost constantly since I started reading. The word 'guide' is thrown about a lot in psychic circles, and although I was aware of help around me, I didn't really know exactly who he/ she/ they/ were. By this point I'd established that it definitely *wasn't* Fred Flintstone!

All the other readers seemed to know who *their* guides were. One of the readers, Carol, even boasted that she had Henry VIII and Dick Turpin, the eighteenth century highway man, as her main guides – God help her! Come back Fred, all is forgiven!

So far, the other readers had told me that I had four Native Americans, three Chinese gentleman, two Nuns, and a Partridge in a Pear Tree – well, maybe not the Partridge, but you get the idea!

This was getting flipping ridiculous.

I decided to ask the down-to-earth Roger for some guidance on the subject. So when we had a quiet patch one rainy afternoon, I approached his table. As usual, he was sitting there doing one of his beloved crosswords.

'Roger, how can I find out who my main guide is?' I asked, sitting opposite him.

'Ask,' he said simply.

'Ask?' I repeated. 'Is it that easy?'

He shrugged. 'Try it and see. What have you got to lose?'

Taking Roger's advice, that evening I put on my Indian-drumming CD (just in case I did have four Indian guides) and sat cross-legged at the end of the bed.

'It would be amazing to see who's working with me,' I appealed softly. 'If it's possible, can you please, *please* show yourself to me?'

Nothing happened.

A bit disappointed, but hardly surprised, I climbed into bed, shut my eyes and snuggled down.

I stirred a little when Andy came to bed, but soon fell asleep again.

Something woke me up.

Hovering a few feet in front of me there was a man. Well, to be more precise, the head and torso of a man.

He looked about forty, had dark hair and a short black beard, and was staring at me out of wise brown eyes. I could see he was wearing a white shirt. He struck me as looking quite continental, maybe Spanish or something, but I suppose he could've just had a tan. After all, they do call the Spiritual Realms 'The Summerlands'!

Totally gobsmacked, I bolted upright. As we eyeballed each other, he slowly faded away, and then reappeared, but slightly further back. This happened three times in total. The room was in semi-darkness, but the whole area around him was surrounded in soft white light. Although by this time I was quite used to seeing strange men in my room (keep it clean, please) I'd never witnessed this disappearing and re-appearing phenomena before – or since! This guy obviously wanted me to get a clear look at him.

When he was gone, I just sat staring at the space he had occupied, all sorts of emotions swirling round inside me.

This was my guide! It had to be. I had asked, and he had shown himself to me! How amazing was that!

To use the words 'humbled' and 'privileged' doesn't come close to describe how I felt at that precise moment.

I realise that some people can ask to they're blue, purple or red in the face, and might not receive anything, and I can't explain why that is; I wish I knew.

I've asked for various things to be shown to me over the years, and they haven't *always* manifested. But, on this one glorious occasion, they did! Who am I to question the hows and the whys? I was just incredibly grateful that my request had been granted.

Excitedly, I woke Andy and started to babble on about my experience.

'Yeah, great! Tell me in the morning,' he muttered sleepily.

God! What *is* it with men and their sleep?

Although I was now a professional reader I still wanted to do everything in my power to develop my abilities to their fullest, so I booked a weekend mediumship course at a farmhouse in Devon.

The advertisement for the course had immediately grabbed my attention. It'd been titled *Come and Learn How to Be a Happy Medium!* Which was exactly what I wanted to be – a happy medium!

Little did I know that I would receive something priceless whilst on this incredible weekend; an amazing gift from Spirit. This gift has sustained me many times over the years, especially when I've found my confidence waning.

It was early evening on the Saturday, and Andy and I had driven to a cosy restaurant for our evening meal. It'd been a fantastic day, full of psychic games and exercises that had really stretched our psychic abilities to their limit. I was really excited because a psychic artist was coming to the farmhouse to give a demonstration that evening. I'd never seen a psychic artist before, but knew people who had, and it sounded awesome.

While we were waiting to be served I suddenly heard a voice in my head.

I nearly fell off my chair. It was Dad's voice. '*I'm going to come through the artist*,' he said matter-of-factly. Then he was gone.

You've got to appreciate that Dad had been in spirit for around five years by now, and I'd heard from him just once. That had only been a quick message for my brother, Steve, which I'll come to a bit later.

In fact, it had been so quiet on the Dad-front, I was beginning to wonder if he'd 'gone downstairs'!

'Are you okay?' Andy enquired, noticing I'd grown quiet – something he wasn't used to!

I nodded and told him what I'd heard.

Andy smiled. 'That'll be nice.'

I waited for Andy to expand on this comment, but he didn't. Andy's always been a man of few words. I sometimes think The Boss Man Himself could appear and Andy would say 'hello' and that would be it!

Back in the car I immediately began to have nagging doubts about what I'd heard. Thank God I didn't have very long to wait to see if Dad *would* keep his promise and come through, as patience isn't a strong trait of mine.

The artist was an elderly lady called Mary who had the wisest, kindest eyes I'd ever seen. As she began sketching the first face she explained to us that the spirit person would draw very close and impress on her how they looked whilst on Earth. She'd then translate that to the canvass. I listened in fascination. It sounded like quite a tricky process to me.

I watched hypnotised as her pencil moved rapidly over the paper. A face of some sorts was definitely forming, but at this point it was difficult to say if it was male or female.

I nudged Andy. 'That's Dad.'

Andy frowned and shook his head in disagreement.

I could see his point. But instinctively I *knew* it was Dad.

I held my breath as before my eyes Dad's very distinct face slowly emerged. First his deep-set dark eyes, then his rather large bulbous nose, followed by his familiar jawline. As Mary was working she was also giving a stream of information about the 'gentleman's character'.

'Does anyone recognise him yet?' She asked, glancing over her shoulder.

'Yes, yes, I do! It's my dad. He told me he would come through and he has!' I then, embarrassingly, burst into loud sobs.

It was so surreal seeing Dad's face appearing like that, especially after his words to me at the restaurant. I told the others about his promise to make an appearance. They were amazed and pleased for me.

'I'm just going to confirm this *is* your father, dear,' Mary said.

I was puzzled. It *was* Dad. How could she confirm it? Then she taught me something I've never forgotten – the difference between a *good* medium and a *great* one. She gave me what I call 'the cherry on top of the cup-cake'.

She wrote a name on the bottom corner on the picture. When I saw it I nearly fainted. It said *'Joan'. Joan is my mum's name.*

How *could* any intelligent person just pooh-pooh that sort of survival evidence? I suppose they would say that Mary copied my face, as I might look like my Dad, but I can assure you that I don't. I take after my mum's side of the family – luckily! Sorry, Dad, no offence, but as you used to say yourself – you were no oil painting! And anyway, how could she have known my mum was Joan? Yes, it's a common enough name, but there are literally hundreds of 'common' names!

Early next morning, I sneaked off by myself and took a stroll around the stunning garden. I felt so peaceful, and – at the risk of sounding like a seventies hippy – at one with the world.

Dad coming through had somehow changed me. It's very hard to explain, but knowing he was well and happy and still looking out for me was an incredible feeling. Very humbling.

More than anything I wanted to be able to make others feel how Mary had made *me* feel.

'Dad,' I whispered. 'I'll work hard to be the best medium I can possibly be. I know I didn't do very much when you were alive to make you proud, but I will now, Dad. I promise you that.'

Back home from Devon, I continued reading at the psychic fairs. I was still struggling Big Time with my nerves. The conflicting advice I received from the other well-meaning readers didn't really help.

At least three of the other readers kept nagging me to get myself a pack of tarot, as, apparently, it would make it a lot easier. But this didn't feel right for me. I was the only one who read without anything; cards, palm, runes, etc., and I think this really puzzled the others. A couple of times I tried Angel cards, but the one off random words just tended to throw me and I just ended up waffling on about the word, which really had no true relevance to the person or their lives. It was just too vague for my liking. So I stuck to listening to the information I was picking up on them psychically, or linking in with their relatives in Spirit.

The other problem I had, apart from my nerves, was that I still felt like an outsider looking in. The other readers were mostly very nice, especially Roger, who'd been very kind and supportive to me, but I got a very strong impression the others weren't exactly sure what I was doing there. I felt very isolated as I watched their easy banter and joking around with each other. For some reason I found it impossible to join in. Deep down I just didn't feel that I deserved to be there. Because I'd started on the aloe vera stall I felt like I'd sneaked in the backdoor to become a reader! It was crazy, but that's how I felt – like I should get back with Andy behind our stall.

But then Helen arrived, and everything changed for me.

5

The Decision

I'd been reading for around four months when Helen turned up with Roger at a fair in Cuffley.

I must admit, I was quite surprised when he introduced Helen as his wife, as I'd assumed she was his daughter. She looked about twenty-five, was very slim, well dressed, and good-looking, with long blonde highlighted hair. Roger is a very nice looking guy (and to be fair owns the most amazing collection of snazzy waistcoats) but I knew he was well into his fifties.

I was very busy that evening, but towards the end of the night when it grew quiet, Helen strolled across to my table. She asked if I was coping better with my nerve-problem (Roger had filled her in). She also mentioned that she wanted to be a reader too, but lacked the confidence.

Within minutes we were chatting away like we'd known each other for years. We just 'clicked'.

A couple of days later she turned up at the next fair in Kent, wearing a very sexy but sophisticated black dress which showed off her slim figure and blonde hair to perfection. I felt really scruffy in comparison in my usual old favourite faded Bag-puss T-shirt and jeans. I must admit I felt a little envious of this glamorous new addition to the fairs.

'I'm reading today, Anne,' she smiled as I went over to say hello.

'Oh, right!' I said, surprised. I carried on unpacking my bits and bobs, feeling a bit peeved. Just a few days ago she had supposedly been thinking about 'possibly becoming a reader in the future', and now here she was glammed up to the nines and happily setting up her table.

Throughout the evening I couldn't help glancing over at her. She seemed really popular, and was doing quite a few readings. I could see she worked like me, without any kind of props.

Pete strode over to my table. 'Helen's getting *amazing* reports about her readings, Anne. You'll have to step it up a gear now you're not the new kid on the block anymore, sweetheart!'

I tried to smile through gritted teeth, but my stomach was churning away with its usual nerves, and something else – something stronger – jealousy!

I had half-hoped she'd be rubbish, but no such luck. Not very spiritual thoughts, I know!

As the fair emptied and we started packing our things away, Helen rushed across the hall to see me. My head was pounding and all I wanted to do was get home to my bed, but I managed a weak smile.

'God, I'm shaking like a leaf,' she murmured, lifting her hand up to show me. 'It's *really, really* nerve-wracking, isn't it? How do you do it week after week?'

She was as pale as a ghost, apart from her chest and neck, which had broken out in the same nervous blotchy rash I suffer from. My childish jealousies melted away as I started at her open, kind face. Her eyes reflected all the fears and anxieties that I felt inside. It was quite eerie – like I was looking in a mirror.

'It does get a bit easier,' I fibbed. 'By the way, I heard you did brilliantly. Well done.'

'I did enjoy it,' she admitted. 'Once I got going I just wanted to do my very best for them.'

I nodded in agreement. Yes – I'd definitely met a soul mate!

I was approaching my thirty-first birthday. Andy and I had been married for over three years, and people kept asking when we were going to start a family. I'd always wanted children, and assumed that we would have them. That's what people do, get married and have kids. All my friends and cousins had.

I really enjoyed being around children, and loved the voluntary work I did running a *Rainbows* group. This is a group that's run by the Girl Guides for girls aged five to seven, which they join before they go up to *Brownies*. I'd done this for about three years, and adored every single second of it.

Andy and I discussed the possibility of kids, but came to the conclusion that whilst we were living at Mum's and were working at the fairs, it was impossible.

We were out at least three evenings a week, and more of less every weekend, and we were still just about surviving financially. Mum was nearly seventy, and couldn't have coped with a baby in the house. It just wasn't practical. Also, I knew if I wanted to continue reading, I wouldn't have the physical or emotional energy to look after a baby. I know plenty probably could, but not me.

I've not been blessed with great health, and have suffered with asthma and numerous allergies since childhood. My energy's limited on the best of days. Realistically, if we wanted a baby Andy would have to get a conventional job, and I'd have to give up my dream of being a medium just as it had started to become a reality!

Andy told me he'd go along with whatever I decided; so what was it to be – Medium or Mum?

Deep down I knew there was no contest. I wanted to continue my spiritual work. There was so much to learn about, so much to experience, so many new people to meet.

But mostly, with every ounce of my soul, I wanted to share this incredible, amazing truth of an afterlife with as many as possible. To let them know their loved ones were well and happy, and that no one needed to fear passing over; something that's much more common than I ever realised!

I wasn't just *telling* people this and expecting them to blindly accept it as 'The Truth'. I was doing my bloody *hardest* to give them *proof*!

Proof, or evidence, is paramount to mediumship. Of course, it's next to impossible to give *ultimate* proof of an afterlife, but in certain conditions, enough information and personal messages can be obtained to give even the most sceptical person 'food for thought'.

Spirit will do their utmost to *prove* they're just as alive as they ever were, and still retain the personality they had when on Earth. I realise some will disagree with this, and that's fair enough, but everything I've experienced and witnessed has led me to the conclusion that an afterlife most definitely exists.

I've even been privileged enough to have glimpses into this incredible world, and I'll share these experiences with you later on. Words are sometimes an extremely frustrating tool when trying to convey an intense feeling or overpowering emotion, but I'll do my very best.

Going back to the Baby Issue, it would be something that'd haunt me for years. I questioned myself almost every day whether I'd really made the right decision.

Andy didn't seem that bothered either way, but I constantly tortured myself. Was I being selfish by denying us the only thing in life that truly matters – family? Ironically, it's being a medium that's taught me this simple truth.

In the back of my mind I used to comfortingly tell myself, 'Oh, well, maybe one day...' But the busier and the more dedicated I've become in my work, the less likely it's looking.

As the months sped by, I continued to read at the fairs. An array of readers would come and go, but there were about eight or nine of us that always seemed to be there.

There was good old Roger and his wife, the gorgeous Helen. And there was Agnes, a platinum blonde lady in her sixties, originally from Hungary. From the stories she told us she'd had the most incredible roller coaster of a life.

Then there was Mystic Baz, a 'larger than life' man, in more than just his huge size. This cockney geezer loved to pretend he was great at conning people, but in truth he really was a good psychic when he put his mind to it. His chat-up line to try and secure himself a reading was a little unconventional. He'd approach the public sitting in the middle of the fair waiting for a demonstration, and ask them if they'd like to feel his balls! He would then produce a dirt-grey pair of rocks, about the size of tennis balls, and tell his captivated audience that they were meteors that had fallen to earth thousands of years ago and were priceless.

Helen and I used to roll our eyes comically at each other, as there were the usual gasps of amazement from the audience. Roger had told us how Baz had purchased them for the grand price of £3.99 from a shop in Brighton.

Mystic Baz's other favourite past time was to show everyone, whether they were interested or not, the huge grinning scar across his abdomen, which he'd acquired when having a gastric-band fitted to help him lose weight.

As they were the two Alfa-males of the group, Baz and Pete clashed Big-Time. It was quite amusing to observe them interacting with each other; like watching two stags-beetles locking horns in mortal combat!

The dark, wild-haired Minnie was another very strong character. She was a tough-talking Londoner, who essentially had a good heart. She laughed like a hyena, and always set everyone else off once she 'got the giggles'. Minnie had given me a bit of a hard time when I'd started reading, and I must admit I was a little wary of her. But after a few months she softened towards me, and had even invited me to her home for a meal – which was very tasty. She was always a bit off with Helen though, which upset me quite a bit.

Then there was the quiet Carol, with her smudging rituals and her dubious collection of guides. And I mustn't forget Sheila, or 'Noddy-Lady', as we affectionately used to call her. Sheila was a very talented artist, and in the sixties she'd worked for the famous children's author, Enid Blyton. She told us that she'd once done some of the artwork for the *Noddy* books. If talking ever became an Olympic sport then Sheila could win gold, no question. If someone sat down with her for a reading you could guarantee they wouldn't emerge for at least two hours. Half an hour was the actual reading, and the rest was about her life story. But no one minded, as she'd had such an interesting life, and had met so many fascinating people. We teased her about it, which she seemed to enjoy. Sheila was one of the most warm-hearted ladies I'd ever met in my life.

Julie, another reader, was a young mum of two, and also a very talented medium. Like me, she'd started off behind a stall, and had progressed to being a reader.

Lastly, there was Rainbow-Man, who wasn't a reader as such. To be honest, I'm not quite sure *what* he used to do. It seemed to mainly consist of running errands for Pete. Rainbow-Man wore the tightest leather trousers imaginable, and had a rather cute bum (which of course I never noticed). Also, he could do things with a pendulum that were pretty mind-boggling!

A bunch of quirky and diverse people I don't think you could find if you tried! Inevitably, there were plenty of squabbles, backbiting, gossiping and jealousy over who was doing the most readings. There was also a huge amount of laughter, fun and jokes (usually told by Roger or Baz) so it all balanced out in the end, as life generally does.

Since Helen's arrival in July I felt much happier. We supported each other when we were nervous – which was pretty much all the time! We'd comforted each other when we'd had a difficult or intense reading, and shared each other's joy when we'd really made a difference and helped someone; whether with their lives, or linking with a loved one.

We would rush off to the loos before the public arrived to plaster on our war paint, and have a good old gossip about our lives. It made such a difference to know that I wasn't the only one shaking with nerves before each venue. It always amazed me that the other readers seemed so laid back and relaxed before a fair, even managing to *eat*! I thing I could never achieve before giving readings, and still can't!

Then again, Helen and I were the two youngest readers, and the others were mostly in their forties or fifties and had been reading for years, and therefore well past the 'nervous stage'.

It finally got to the point where I was so blooming fed-up of feeling like a wobbling petrified jelly, full of nerves and tension before each fair, that I decided to Take Action!

Someone mentioned to me that they had found hypnotherapy really helpful in managing anxiety, so I decided to make an appointment with a hypnotherapist!

We'd meet this very nice Indian man called Gurdip whilst we'd been with Adrian's fairs. I knew he had a good reputation as a hypnotist, so I made an appointment with him. Andy drove me to his house in South London on a very wet and miserable Saturday afternoon. Gurdip gave me a warm welcome hug, then showed me into his spacious front room.

Nervously, I took a seat, wondering if it was too late to back out. Hypnosis has always made me feel a little uneasy.

In the early nineties I'd gone to see Paul McKenna's stage show three or four times, and found it really difficult to believe the things people did whilst they were under hypnosis. I had these visions of myself clucking like a demented hen, or milking an invisible cow, or worse!

'Shut your eyes and just relax your mind,' Gurdip instructed in soothing dulcet tones. 'I'm going to take you through a little relaxation exercise. Now, I want you to focus on your toes, feel them melting away, completely relaxing.'

My toes *were* relaxed until I'd had to focus on them. Now I could feel them tensing up in rebellion.

This went on until he'd reached the top of my head, by which point I was a complete and utter shivering wreck.

The whole process and taken about half an hour, which meant half my allocated time was gone already. I hoped the hypnotherapy bit was coming up soon. This session was costing me an arm and a leg. (Even if it *was* a very relaxed arm and leg!)

'*Now you are completely relaxed,*' Gurdip suddenly boomed, making me jump out of my skin. '*Listen very carefully to what I'm telling you. You are a calm, confident person. You are capable of handling any situation you are presented with. All the tension and stress inside you is draining away. You are a happy, strong, amazing person...*'

I felt myself drifting off as Gurdip carried on in this vein for another few minutes. Suddenly I was aware of the sharp snapping of fingers.

'How do you feel, Anne?' he inquired after he'd 'woken me up'.

I nodded. 'Fine.' I wasn't sure what I'd been expecting, but somehow I felt a little cheated. I thought I would waltz in, and he would somehow wave a wand and magic away all my fears and nerves. He *might* have for all I knew, but I wouldn't know for sure until I was at the next fair. That was the *real* test. But in all honestly at that moment I didn't really feel any different.

'How did it go?' asked Andy as I climbed in the car.

I shrugged. 'Oh, you know... It was okay.'

Andy raised his eyebrows, but made no comment as we drove home.

I didn't have long to wait to find out about the results of the hypnotherapy. We had a fair the following day at a hotel in Newbury.

As I set up my table I did feel a lot less anxious than

usual. Gurdip's words were swirling round and round my mind; *You are calm, confident and in control of the situation.* I carefully placed my array of crystals around my table. *You control your nerves, they do not control you.* I took out my comments book and leaflets. *Nothing fazes you.*

This was fantastic! I could really do this. I was actually looking forward to reading today rather than experiencing the usual feelings of absolute dread. Yes, my stomach still felt a little churned up, but it was manageable.

The day went very well. I had a couple of 'wibbly-wobbly moments' but Gurdip was there just like a tiny tape-recording in my head, encouraging me and egging me on, telling me I could do it, like a supportive parent or best mate.

The effects of the hypnosis lasted a week or so before they unfortunately wore off. Before I knew it I had regressed to my normal bundle-of-nerves self. I would've been very nice to have had a few more sessions, but money was just too tight to justify it.

The other experience I've had with hypnosis was at a sleepy fair in Bexley. Everyone was bored rigid. It was after 2pm and for some reason no one had turned up. The atrocious weather had obviously put people off. Roger called all of us over to the seating area in the middle of the hall. He had a cheeky smile on his face as he explained he wanted to take us on an inner-journey.

Half the readers rolled their eyes as nervous giggles rippled round the group. Mystic Baz laughed loudly, and made a comment regarding a recent 'inner-journey' he'd taken with some lucky lady. Everyone ignored him, used to his crude humour.

'I'm going to take you on a journey to your past-life,' Rog said intriguingly. 'Shut your eyes and breathe deeply.'

I did as instructed, but inwardly I sighed. *Here we go again*! I thought negatively. *This is where everyone gets fabulous stuff and I get nothing.*

But as I followed Roger's instructions, I was suddenly transported to a really pretty park. Looking around, I could see people strolling by. Someone rode past me on a strange-looking bicycle. I recognised it as a penny-farthing. I was aware all this was happening in my mind, but it was such an incredibly real experience. I could feel the sun beating down on the back of my head, and could hear the laughter of children nearby. I looked down at myself. I was wearing a filthy old pair of trousers and a well-worn grey jacket.

The fact I was a man only mildly surprised me. I knew my name was Albert, and I was a very miserable, bitter man. My leg ached. In my vision I bent down and rubbed it. It had been damaged in an accident. I don't know how I knew this, but I did.

Roger's soft voice invaded my vision, telling us it was time to return to the room.

Wow! Double wow! What an experience *that* was! I must admit I was a bit miffed that I wasn't Joan of Arc, as I'd been told by Carol. Oh well, I could live with that!

After this experience I had one of my little chats on the subject of reincarnation with my spirit friends. I got the impression from our talk that if we wish to return to Earth we can. However, if we decide that we've had quite enough and don't want to do it again, then that's also fine. When we are between our various physical lives we receive all the help and guidance we need whilst making all these important decisions on what we want our Soul to experience next.

I also asked my guides about the common idea that if we were really bad or cruel to someone would we have to come back and make up for it in a future life on Earth? Surprisingly, I was informed that that's just not the case at all. Apparently, when the parties involved meet in Spirit, it's all discussed and worked-out over there, so when we come back down, it's always with a clean slate, so to speak. All these theories are based on my own private conversations with my spirit friends, and I realise others will have different views on this complicated subject. But to me it makes sense. Why would an innocent new- born baby have to bear the responsibility of what he/she did or didn't do in a completely different life?

I suppose when you think about it, everything regarding religion and the after-life, and such, are just *ideas*. No one, *without question,* on this side of life really understands how any of it truly works until we are there experiencing it for ourselves. If anyone tells you *they've* got all the answers I would suggest one thing – stick on your trainers and run a mile – or at least as far as your fitness level allows!

But what we *can* do is take our own experiences along with our common sense and draw up certain conclusions based upon them. Then, if people wish, share these conclusions with each other.

One day, we were at a fairly quiet fair near Addlestone when a lady in her late thirties apprehensively approached my table. She seemed very nervous and kept glancing over at the entrance as if she was expecting someone unpleasant to appear at any moment.

'I don't want a reading, just a quick word, please,' she almost whispered to me.

I gestured for her to take a seat and asked how I could help. Nervously She fidgeted with her long necklace, her large, dark eyes scanning my face.

'Can you lift curses?' she blurted out at last.

Whatever I expected her to say it wasn't that! 'Lift *curses*?' I repeated in disbelief.

'Yes. I've got a curse on me and desperately need help. Can you do it? If not, do you know anyone who can?'

It did briefly cross my mind that this might be some sort of wind-up, but her earnest face showed me that she was deadly serious. To my horror she burst into loud heartbreaking sobs. 'Please can you help me? I'm desperate!'

She went on to explain that she'd upset some lady who,

supposedly, had super-psychic powers, and this woman had subsequently 'cursed' her.

From that point on, this poor lady told me that a series of incidents had taken place, getting progressively worse, which seemed to confirm to her that she was indeed under some sort of curse.

I wasn't buying it. I had to admit that *yes*, she *had* had a lot of bad luck, but under a curse...

What upset me more than anything – and makes my blood boil when I even think about it – is that she'd been to see two other psychic ladies, who had taken money off her (I don't know how much) and had told her the curse would soon be lifted. But the bad luck seemed to get even worse after she'd consulted them.

Now, she really felt she was losing her mind, and had decided to come to the psychic fair as a final go at 'freeing' herself.

Frankly I was totally amazed she'd ever want to see a psychic again as long as she lived, but here she was putting her trust in me. I just wasn't sure how to go about helping her.

I asked my spirit team if they had any words that might be of any use to her. Straight away I was told that the curse had indeed affected her life, which really shocked me.

My guide explained it was *because* she believed in this wretched curse so strongly that she was encountering all these problems.

This wasn't the case to begin with.

One bad thing involving her career had happened, and after that it'd been a downward spiral connected with finances and her relationship. Now, the belief was so deeply ingrained in her after the string of events she'd experienced, she was *expecting* bad things to happen – and they were. By focusing on the stupid bloody curse she was giving it power.

It was a 'catch 22' situation. I was a bit puzzled about

why the bad stuff hadn't stopped after she'd paid the two other psychics. If it was happening on a sub-conscious level, *why hadn't it stopped when she'd thought the curse had been lifted*? A bit of digging and I found out that she didn't have much faith in the other two psychics' 'power' compared to the lady who'd *originally* 'cursed' her.

I did my very best to explain what I thought was happening to her, but she didn't look very convinced. I felt so frustrated as I knew her belief that was cursed was so *incredibly* strong in her mind she'd have to wait for someone 'powerful' to come along and 'release' her from it (probably releasing her of a lot of money at the same time). There was no way she'd accept it if I told her that she had the power to release herself at any time she wanted.

I think possibly that this could be quite a common occurrence, although the only other time I've heard of something a little similar to this was from a friend of mine called Jimmy.

Jimmy was an American guy I met on a mediumship course a few years back.

One day I received a call out the blue from him. He'd been to see a psychic-medium to see if she could advise him on a financial matter – personally, I would've recommended a financial adviser! She'd told him to bury a certain amount of money under a particular tree on a particular date at midnight.

On hearing this I thought I must have a build-up of wax in my ears or something, and asked him to repeat it! This was completely *crazy* stuff! He was *out* of his tree if he followed this advice.

He admitted rather sheepishly that he *had* already done it!

I lost contact with him shortly after this call, so will never know if it did enhance his financial situation, but I doubt it somehow – although the psychic's were enhanced, I'm sure!

One evening, Pete informed us it was his fiftieth coming up and we were all invited to his birthday-bash, being held at a casino in Reading.

This was the first time we had all met up socially, so I took great care getting all dolled up, as the others had only ever seen me in T-shirt and jeans.

It was really lovely to hear all their compliments, and the evening went very well. We were in the middle of this fantastic meal, when Pete suddenly told us he'd been born in 1950. But that made him 49, surely?

Somehow he'd managed to gain a year. Pete couldn't be happier when it dawned on him he was actually a year younger than he thought. How he'd managed to get it wrong is amazing, especially as it was easy to calculate as he was born in 1950! Shows how scatty we mediums can be!

We had a good laugh about it, and then set about the real business of the evening – hitting the roulette tables!

'This should be fun,' I grinned at Helen. 'Twelve psychics playing the roulette wheel. Ha! They won't know what's hit 'em!'

An hour later and we'd all lost money! Huh, flipping good bunch of psychics we were!

We left, tail between our legs, muttering to the amused staff about how we couldn't use our powers for excessive personal gain.

A week or so after our trip to the casino, I had a one-day psychic course booked at a hall near Staines. What I didn't realise (as I hadn't read the leaflet properly) was that the course was geared up for people who had strong artistic ability, and wanted to use it to link with Spirit. Yes, I can draw a stick-person quite well, but an artist I'm most definitely not.

The tutor, a tall elegant lady in a flowing dress, started to pass around the drawing-paper and a various array of paints and charcoals. I started to panic. It dawned on me that this was a bunch of trainee psychic artists, like Mary, who'd drawn Dad.

'Do you paint?' the lady sitting next to me inquired.

I shrugged, non-committedly, wondering if our spare bedroom I'd painted last month would count.

'I specialise in mythological people and creatures, but I thought this course would open my mind to higher Spiritual Souls, Angelic Beings and that. I would love to capture them on canvas.'

I nodded, thinking of my stick-people. They would be about as welcome here as a juicy sirloin steak at a vegetarian's convention!

The lady, Janet, proceeded to show me her portfolio. My God, this lady was sooo talented. I felt like getting up and sneaking off home before I made a complete fool of myself. I'm so glad I didn't.

The first exercise we did was a guided meditation, not my favourite thing as you know, but surprisingly it went really well. I could clearly see in my mind's eye the man who had appeared in my room a few months previously.

'Your guide is giving you a gift,' the tutor told us softly.

As she said this I saw a beautiful shinning ruby being pressed into my palm.

'Can I ask your name?' I asked.

He nodded. '*It's Honrad.*'

I thought I'd heard it wrong, so got him to repeat it. No, he definitely said *Honrad*.

Bit of a weird name, but I wasn't going to argue with him. I'd always been a little sceptical of guides with wacky names, and believe me I've come across a fair few over the years. Why couldn't they be called George, or Sid, or Ethel? And here I was with a Honrad! Well, one thing is for sure – there was no way my mind would've come up with *that* one, so I'm pretty sure it was from a spiritual source.

When we 'came back' we were handed a small piece

of card and asked to draw our gift and keep it nearby to inspire us. I drew my ruby, which luckily was fairly easy, and kept it with me for years after. It really did (and still does) help me to feel connected to Honrad when I feel a little lost or low.

The other thing that came from this course was that I sent off for a picture of one of my guides, drawn by the tutor. When I got it back it was of a young lady, with long flowing hair, called Rosella. I didn't have a clue who this guide was, and suspect, with all due respect, that it was a figment of the artist's imagination. Nevertheless, I displayed it on my table at the fairs, and was told quite often that I resembled Rosella. Maybe she was a long-lost ancestor of mine!

Although from a reading point of view the fairs were going brilliantly for me, there was a lot of unsettlement amongst the readers with the way things were being run.

Pete was booking fairs at the same old venues too regularly. He was also booking in too many readers, so there wasn't enough readings to go round. It was so awful sitting there and competing with twelve other readers for the smattering of people milling round trying to decide who to choose to see. It seriously damaged many a good reader's ego, mine included, and in the early days I used to often sit there and question why I hadn't been 'chosen'.

Another thing that happened was that sometimes we would turn up for a fair only to find that it'd been cancelled, but Pete had forgotten to phone us to let us know. When you've spent all day mentally preparing yourself, and then driven for an hour or longer, it was very annoying and stressful – although secretly I was always quite relieved.

Once we turned up at a fair only to find it totally deserted. We called Pete and he told us it'd been cancelled. He asked if we would kindly stick up a notice to inform the other readers and the public of the situation.

Andy found a piece of paper and began to scribble a

note. Grinning, he showed it to me:

Psychic fair cancelled – due to unforeseen circumstances. Sorry for any inconvenience.

Someone obviously found it amusing because it ended up being reported in the local paper! I don't think Pete was very impressed though – whoops! Poor Andy wasn't his favourite person after that!

Pete also had a superb talent at winding people up. He exploded with alarming regularity. Everyone felt unsettled when he was about. I was incredibly grateful to him for pushing me in at the 'deep-end', but felt annoyed when he kept telling anyone who'd listen that he taught me everything I knew!

That was rubbish. My spirit friends were the ones who'd supported and guided me with my work.

One evening, Roger and Helen had invited us to dinner at their bungalow in Worthing. Helen had told me that there was something top-secret they wanted to discuss with us.

Feeling pretty stuffed after a very tasty meal Roger had cooked us, the 'Top Secret' information was finally revealed.

'Baz and I are taking over the running of the fairs,' Roger told us as we sipped our coffee. 'Pete has agreed to sell them to us. We'll be taking over in January.'

I felt so relieved. Over the last six months Andy had done a lot of work for Pete, taking over the advertising of the venues, and other little bits and bobs. We had even found three or four new venues for him which had been really successful. All Andy got in return was a free table for the aloe vera, which would've been ten pounds. It wasn't very much for the hours Andy was putting in for Pete.

Roger and Baz still wanted Andy to help out, and had worked out a much fairer deal for him.

And so the new millennium began, and things were a little more harmonious than they'd been. It was quite amusing because Minnie (who'd treated Helen like a leper before the take-over) was now acting as if she was her best mate in the Whole-Wide-World. Yes, the pecking order had definitely changed!

I was sitting at my table feeling more than a little queasy, and beginning to regret the Indian take-away we'd had the previous night. We were at a busy Sunday fair at Hemel Hempstead, and I had three or four people on my waiting list. When I finished them, I slipped off to the toilets just to get my breath back.

I bumped into Helen in the corridor. 'Are you all right?' she asked.

'Not great,' I admitted, leaning against the wall.

'Go and see the healer we've got in today,' she suggested. 'He's supposed to be really good.'

I hadn't had much experience of healing – apart from being told half a dozen times that I would be good at it. I was a little dubious about this because it'd never really held my interest. The healers that often attended the fairs just seemed to shut their eyes and stand behind their patient. If they were feeling particularly ambitious, they might mystically wave their arms about a little, but that was it – or so I thought. How wrong could you be!

6

My First Demonstration

'Please come in,' the man called out, as I knocked timidly on the door.

With trepidation, I entered the tiny side-room the healer was using.

'Hop up on the bed and I'll see what we can do for you,' he smiled, pointing to the therapist-couch.

'I'm Tony, by the way. Now, just relax and get yourself comfy. Have you had healing before?' Tony was vigorously rubbing his hands together as he was chattering away to me. This was a little worrying! *Why does he need to warm up his hands*? My mind was furiously thinking.

He placed his hands about six inches over my face. 'Don't worry, I'm not going to touch you,' he explained, obviously seeing my worried face. 'I'm just gently sending healing energy to you via my hands.'

Almost immediately I experienced this really strong tingling sensation over my whole face, like intense pins and needles.

'Can you feel anything, Anne?'

'Yes. God, that's amazing!'

How he was doing this I couldn't tell you. Truthfully, I'm a very sceptical person, but this was a definite physical sensation. Like a very mild electric-charge gently caressing me.

As he slowly moved his hands, the tingling sensations continued. I felt incredible relaxed and at peace with the world. It was such a wonderful floaty kind of feeling; exactly what I needed to soothe my stressed mind and ease my painful stomach.

Twenty minutes later I sat up and thanked Tony for the marvellous healing. I hadn't felt so good in months.

'You're welcome, my dear,' he grinned. 'Oh, by the way, did you sense my guide?'

'No,' I admitted.

Tony shrugged. 'No matter. Not many people do.'

His next words shocked me, and made me doubt everything I'd just experienced.

'My guide was from another planet when he was in physical form. He resembles a giant lizard.'

I was totally stunned. *Oh my God,* this man was a complete and utter fruit-loop. He was sitting there telling me he had a seven-foot reptile for a guide! He'd obviously been watching too many episodes of *Star Trek*. This put Carol and her Dick Turpin to shame!

I felt my blood begin to boil. Tony was *exactly* the sort of person that gave everything I was trying to do a bad name. No wonder people were sceptical about the existence of the spiritual realms with idiots like him about. Tony gave the doubting Joe's ammunition by the bucket load to throw at us psychics.

At home, I asked Honrad about Tony and his so-called intergalactic lizard guide.

In my mind's eye I was suddenly looking down on planet Earth.

Then the scene zoomed out and I was aware of the entire Solar System.

Zooooom... I was now gazing in awe at the entire galaxy.

Zooooom... a thousand swirling galaxies.

Zooooom... an infinite number of swirly colourful galaxies.

Words flowed clearly through my mind:

Why would all this be created for no reason? Life is abundant throughout the Universe in many forms.

The spiritual realms aren't exclusively for Earth-people. Souls from other worlds are given the opportunity to help people different to themselves, if they so choose. Think of it as a universal foreign-exchange programme.

The incredible scene dissolved and I opened my eyes.

Well – that had told me!

I felt quite ashamed of myself. I had judged Tony and dismissed him as a total fruit-cake. Of all people I knew what it felt like to be judged for having unconventional beliefs. People were constantly judging me for talking to 'dead people'.

I'm not saying we should believe every single thing presented to us, but before dismissing something as impossible, it should be given a little thought that maybe, just maybe, it could be the truth.

That's not always the case though. I've had quite a few readings that really have been pure nonsense.

About fifteen years ago, I was told by a medium at a church service that I would have a 'breath-taking vision of Heaven' reflected in a teaspoon. (Every time I make a brew I always have a quick peek at the spoon, but so far no vision!)

I've had quite a few readings that have mostly consisted of what I call psychic-babble. One lady spent the entire reading informing me that my chakras needed a good cleansing and re-balancing (at quite a cost). I asked her why and she muttered a load of would-be clever words, that sounded dead impressive, but in truth was absolute tommyrot.

Another reading I had, which quite shocked me, was when an elderly psychic told me that I would never get cancer!

At the time I felt pleased, but after the reading, when I'd time to think about it, I couldn't believe how irresponsible it was to say I'd never get cancer. What if I was the sort of person that really took this as gospel and never checked myself for lumps or whatever? No one on the face of the planet can make such a claim about such an important issue. Also, the lady in question didn't give me one name or personal detail of any significance, although she kept repeating what a great person I was, obviously trying to appeal to my ego.

I've always felt that just one relevant piece of information, such as a name or important date, is worth all the flattery and psychic-babble in the entire world.

In my opinion, psychic-babble makes it all so complicated, and blurs the real truth, beauty and simplicity of Spirit.

As I wanted this to be a 'warts-and-all' book, I wanted to share with you the most terrible reading I've ever heard about:

An extremely distraught lady turned up at a psychic fair in Hampshire. She told us she'd had a tarot reading at another psychic fair and had been informed that her son was going to be involved in a fatal car-accident within the year.

It's quite hard to believe that such things could actually be said within a reading, but according to this lady, they were. She obviously wanted some sort of advice or reassurance that this tragic information wasn't true.

I didn't speak to her personally on this matter, but the ones that did talk to her managed to calm her down and reassure her that this sort of information wouldn't be given willy-nilly by the spirit world.

We never heard from her again, so I don't know if this terrible prediction ever did occur. God, I really hope not.

It was around this time Andy started to get interested in numerology.

This is a little bit like astrology, but is based around your birth name and date. I was more than a little sceptical about it, as astrology and that type of thing have never really sat comfortably with me. I have many friends who are very much into astrology, and at the risk of upsetting them, and no doubt many other people, I find it all rather vague.

I've had many professional charts done over the years, but have found some of the information applied and some didn't. Even the information that applied was ambiguous. Sorry, but not good enough.

Andy was convinced that there was something in it though. (And he was the non-believer when we met!) So I kept my mouth shut and let him get on with it. He only did the odd couple of numerology charts a week, but he enjoyed giving his talks on it at the fairs, and it was something different from the usual readings on offer.

Ah yes – the dreaded 'talks'. As readers we were all expected to give a short talk, and then demonstrate our various abilities, whether it was our Talents with the Tarot, or the Powers of Palm-reading, or our Cleverness at Clairvoyance. Pete had never really pushed me into doing a talk. He'd just let the readers get up and give a talk if they were at a loose end and wanted to try and conjure up some interest that would hopefully lead to a reading.

I'd never volunteered. Doing a one-to-one reading was stressful enough, but the thought of standing in front of an audience with all those staring, goggling eyes...

No thank you.

Roger was pretty good and left me alone for a few months. But one Sunday afternoon he approached my table, his mouth set in a determined line.

'Can you give a talk in a minute, Anne?'

I glanced over at the thirty of so people sitting in the middle of the hotel room. Some of them were looking around in expectation, obviously waiting for the next demonstration to begin. My heart started to beat so rapidly I thought it might burst out my chest. Quick! Pass the paper bag someone!

Roger sat down and smiled gently at me. 'You can't avoid it forever, love. Everyone has to give a talk at some point. Even Helen did one this morning. You're the only one who hasn't done one yet.'

Fiddlesticks! I thought no one had noticed.

'Just link with one or two spirits. You're a cracking little medium, and it's much easier working with a large audience than giving a one-to-one once you've overcome the nerves.'

'But I've never worked in front of an audience before,' I

whined, sounding like a five-year-old not wanting to go to school on a Monday morning. 'I've not even spoken to an audience about anything in my life, let alone made a link.'

Roger looked a little impatient. 'Come on, Anne, give it a go. Just ten minutes, okay?'

I nodded in resignation. 'I'll just nip to the loo first.'

On my way, I beckoned wildly over at Helen to follow me.

In 'the office', as we called our panic-meetings in the Ladies, I asked if she had any tips for me. If she hadn't then I might just consider booking a plane ticket and leaving the country – pronto!

'Try psychometry with them if you're worried about mediumship,' Helen suggested. 'Get someone to give you a ring or watch and see what you pick up. Then get them to try it on each other. It's good fun and not as daunting as linking with a spirit.'

I could've kissed Helen. She understood my fears completely and had offered me an easier alternative. What would we do without good, supportive mates in the world, huh?

Praying for my spirit team to draw close, I took the longest walk of my life from the Ladies back to the hotel room.

My audience was awaiting...

Roger introducing me in his booming voice as 'one of the best psychics he'd ever encountered' didn't really help with my thumping heart and churning tummy.

I appreciate the sentiments, but No Pressure now you've said that Rog!

I noticed that most of the other readers weren't working but were sitting at their tables round the room, watching me with great interest, probably wondering what I would do. Agnes had even got out her sandwich box and was happily munching her way through her usual cheese and pickle. Minnie was peering expectantly at me over the rim of her plastic coffee cup.

I wouldn't have been surprised if Mystic Baz had suddenly appeared selling flipping choc-ices and popcorn!

God, this is awful. Please stop gawking at me! I thought frantically.

I had often watched the others demonstrating without a second thought, but now the boot was on the other foot, and it felt like a bloody great size 13 boot at that.

'Hi, I'm Anne, and I'm a psychic medium.'

Yes, they already knew that.

This is where I was praying that the proverbial hole in the floor would appear and swallow me up. Who in their right mind would want to be a medium?

Everywhere I looked there were eyes staring in expectation at me, waiting for me to perform.

My mind went utterly and spectacularly blank.

I wasn't born with the gift of the gab like some of the others, so I couldn't blag my way out of this. I could maybe do a little dance instead. Or sing a song or two? No, maybe not – I'm tone deaf. Tell a few smutty jokes? Well, why not? It worked for Mystic Baz!

I glanced over at Helen and she gave me an encouraging smile and pointed to her ring.

Right, yes, the psychometry. Concentrate.

'Has anyone heard of psychometry?' I squeaked, sounding like a mouse on helium.

'Can you speak up, love,' called an elderly lady sitting near the back. So I tried again.

'Psychometry is used as a good way of picking up information about someone,' I explained. 'All the sensitive has to do is hold an object the person has had contact with; jewellery's ideal as it tends to hold onto the energy of the person wearing it.'

Blank faces stared up at me. I could feel my face, neck and chest growing hotter and redder, by the second. By now I knew I was doing a very passable impression of a post-box.

'Would anyone like to give me a piece of jewellery or a watch so I can demonstrate what I mean?'

A lady in the front row took off a plain black wristwatch and waved it at me.

I grasped it in my hand, concentrating on the thoughts, feelings and images immediately penetrating my mind. The eyes staring at me seemed to fade away as I placed all my energy on the watch.

'I'm aware of singing, specifically opera singing.'

'I *do* sing opera,' the lady said in surprise. A murmur rippled round the audience. She certainly didn't look like an opera singer. I was chuffed. That was quite an unusual piece of evidence.

So far so good! 'I'm also aware of walking along a beach with two small dogs.'

The lady nodded. 'Yes, I live by the sea. I'm staying at my sister's this weekend. I've only got one dog though. But sometimes I take out my neighbour's dog.'

More nods and noises of approval came from the audience.

'I can see a nurse's outfit, and I'm seeing blue, which to me symbolises healing. Oh, and books, I'm seeing piles of books.'

The ladies eyes were growing larger by the second. 'I was a nurse until I retired last year. And I absolutely *love* my reading. I read constantly. How are you getting all this from my watch?'

'I'm just allowing the information to flow through me. Your watch has a lot of your energy imprinted on it and I'm just picking it up.'

I was aware that this answer was a little vague, but in truth, I'm not quite sure of the technicalities of *how* I was getting this stuff from the watch, I just was!

Next, an attractive, smartly dressed lady of around forty eagerly handed me a pretty sapphire ring.

An overwhelming sense of loss washed over me and I immediately felt like I wanted to burst into tears. I almost handed her back the ring, but thought that might look a little sinister if I refused to read for her.

The initial feelings of pain soon faded though, and the name Robert 'popped' into my mind.

This is how I obtain most of my information; it just 'pings' into my mind.

The name Robert was accompanied with a sense of a young man who passed extremely suddenly. I stopped focusing on the ring. It was unimportant. This, I realised, was a spirit person drawing close.

'I'm getting the name Robert, Rob.'

The lady looked quite shocked. 'That's my brother.'

'I don't think he's been gone very long. It's a very recent passing. And he went with his heart.'

'Yes. I didn't think he would come through so soon. He only passed three months ago.'

'He's showing me a lorry.'

'Rob was a long-distance lorry drive,' the lady told me. He had a heart-attack whilst driving.'

'Can you take Kitty or Kathy?'

'Kathy. That's mum. Some people call her Kitty. She's alive.'

'Robert sends his love to her. And he's mentioning the boys? There are two sons.'

The lady nodded. She was in tears. This was getting a bit much for her. I could tell Rob was a very quiet man, but understandably, he had so much he wanted to tell his sister, so much to catch up on, but I didn't really want to turn this into a full-blown reading. It was literally a five minute job. In my mind I thanked Robert.

By this point I remember that I was shaking like a jelly on top of a spin-dryer. Spirit hadn't let me down, but working in front of an audience was so incredibly daunting to me. I knew I was probably losing a lot of the evidence and messages that I would get in a one to one.

The evidence I'd achieved was good solid stuff. Nothing mind-blowing, that was for sure, but the two recipients had understood and accepted the information – and that was enough for a short demonstration.

On reflection, I don't believe that the initial feelings of loss I experienced when I'd first held the sapphire ring had anything whatsoever to do with holding it. It was Rob drawing close. He was sharing with me what his family had been feeling since his passing.

I have a theory (which I know most psychics disagree with) that most information sensitives 'pick-up' using tools such as psychometry, is really spirit people and guides drawing close, and projecting 'evidence' into the mediums mind. The objects themselves are not really that important.

To pick up from the vibes coming off a watch that someone is an opera singer seems a little strange. At the time I believed the information *was* from the watch, and possibly it was, but the longer I've been practising this work, the more I feel our spirit friends are there helping us to pick up information. That's how it works for me, anyway, although I do know personal information *is* stored in the auric field, and some do work in this way when gathering their evidence, rather than working with spirit people.

Yes, some of it does seem a little obscure. Why would dead people hang around to tell me that someone likes to sing opera and walk their dog by the sea? But these little 'titbits' *are* important. They switch a light on in people's minds. It might start off as a teeny-weenie little pin-prick of light, which over time, hopefully, will grow to a huge flaming ball.

'How did you know that?'

'How is that possible?'

'How did you do it?'

These are phrases that people have often said to me, and it's always music to my ears. It means I've succeeded in either igniting that light, or building a slightly brighter one.

Of course certain sceptics would say that we'd done our research on the person, and that's how we were getting our information, but that's nonsense. We had no idea who was coming to the fair for a reading, and even if I see someone at home I've usually only got a first name and a mobile number. Believe me; it would not be worth the time and effort involved. Certain magicians replicate *some* of what they *think* mediums do, and I haven't a clue how they do it. Of course there's trickery of some sort involved, but to suggest we all work along those lines is again ridiculous. And then there's the talk of the good old cold reading. Yes, I have heard of and have experienced many vague, could apply to anyone, type readings. We all have. It's old hat.

But what about *truly* specific stuff that could *not* be guessed under *any* circumstances. That's the stuff I (and many others I know) aim for, and most of the time get. If not, what's the point of doing it?

In the course of a reading, not all the information will be amazing, but there *should* be enough 'un-guessable' and very specific information passed on to make any person think deeply about our true spiritual nature.

The quality of evidence can, and of course does, vary with each spirit communication. I've spent many hours analysing why this is, and I'm still not completely sure of the answer.

Most people do receive a very good, solid reading, but for some it can be an *incredible* experience. It seems to be connected to a question of *need*. I've found the more the evidence, which brings such comfort and reassurance, is needed, the more spirit will pull all the stops out, so to speak, to try and deliver that comfort.

Going back to my demonstration, I clearly remember this link with Robert and with the opera-singer lady, as it was my first attempt of mediumship in front of an audience.

Since my departure from the fairs, I haven't pursued platform or stage mediumship in any form. I think it's a really fantastic thing to do, but it's not personally for me. To this day, Roger often asks me if I want to attend a Spiritualist church clairvoyance evening with him to demonstrate, but I always decline. Unless someone physically drags me up onto a platform, I'll happily carry on doing my one-to-ones!

I admire anyone who does have the courage to do this sort of mediumship, but I also want any aspiring slightly shyer mediums out there to know that you can do just one-to-ones and have a very satisfying career.

Back at the relative safety of my table, Rob's sister came over to thank me for the messages from him. She also booked a date with me for a private psychic party.

I'd been reading at the fairs for just over a year at this point, and had been slowly invited to quite a few people's houses to read for themselves and their friends and families.

I saw this as a massive privilege. To be able to go and do four or five readings without the added stress of having to find table-rent, however many readings you actually do, was fantastic. It was also a relief not having the pressure of the natural competitiveness between the readers, and anxiety of the dreaded talk. It was so nice to be able to give each person as long as they needed, because you didn't have people on your waiting list nervously checking their watches in case the evening ended before they'd had a chance to have their reading.

Even the absence of the silly things – like the half hour setting up the table, and the bickering with the others to secure an electricity source, was pure bliss.

I could put *all* my available energy into the readings, which is how it should be. I did around three or four parties a month, which I was hoping to increase to a point where I could give up the fairs and focus just on them instead. I also had many people who wanted to see me at my home, but as I didn't *have* my own home, it wasn't really possible.

I dreamt constantly of us having our own home, where I could perhaps have a cosy little room, dedicated completely to my spiritual work. But what with property prices it was an impossible dream. Or so I thought...

7

Past Lives And Time-Slips...

In September 2000 Mum, Andy and I moved from Dad's Dream House in Guildford.

Mum had decided that we all needed our own space, and, to our amazement, incredibly and generously had offered to give us my inheritance early. I would get a third of the value of the house, and Mum would use the rest to buy a cosy bungalow just outside Guildford. Andy and I could only get a tiny mortgage as our income was so low, but we just managed to get a good deal on an Edwardian semi in Bognor Regis which needed a fair bit of re-modernising. It would've been nice to have stayed near Mum and my brothers and friends in Guildford, but with property prices so high in that area, it was impossible. Also, Helen and Roger lived in Worthing, which is very close to Bognor, and Helen and I were fast becoming best mates. The other benefit was the lovely sea air, which I knew would help my asthma.

Another massive factor was that Dad had always had a thing about Bognor. He loved his Guildford house, but ultimately, if he hadn't passed over I know that one day he would've wanted to move to Bognor. I wanted to fulfil that dream for him.

So, after a couple of months in Essex, staying with Andy's parents as all the details were finalised, we moved into our lovely semi in Bognor.

The joy of putting your key in the door and knowing you (all right, and the building society) own that property, is amazing. Andy had owned a flat, but this was my first property. It was true that we would have a lot more travelling to do, as most of the fairs were nearer to Guildford, but that didn't matter – for the moment, anyhow.

The first night in our new home turned out to be quite an experience for me.

Like many people, I've never been able to sleep the first night in a strange place. At least Andy was enjoying himself, snoring his head off.

Frustrated I couldn't settle, I turned away from the racket next to me, only to be faced with a young man dressed in an army uniform, staring down intently at me. He was clutching some type of rifle, which was a bit worrying! To this day I can vividly remember this solider, with his light blue eyes that seemed to be trying to penetrate my soul. I was used to seeing people at this point (although it *always* takes me by surprise) but normally they drift off or fade away after a few seconds.

Not this guy. Oh, no – he seemed to be going *nowhere*!

'*Who are you*?' I yelled in panic when at last I'd managed to find my voice.

No answer, but at least he disappeared at the sound of my voice.

Andy didn't even stir he was in such a deep sleep.

This soldier appeared to me three times over the next two weeks. In my experience it's so rare that I see the same person more than once. I asked my spirit team about this young solider, and was told he used to live in our house, which is Edwardian. He wasn't haunting it or anything; he was just being nosy and checking out the new owners. (I'm still not quite sure why he'd brought his flipping rifle with him though!)

Another amazing thing that occurred the first week in our own home happened to Andy. He told me about it over breakfast.

'Your dad woke me up this morning,' he said very casually, tucking into his scrambled egg on toast.

'Pardon me?' I said, thinking I might still be in bed and dreaming.

I was just lying there and I heard his voice as clear as

anything, saying; '*Hello, Andy*!'

'You mean you heard him inside your head?' I asked curiously.

'No. I heard him as if he was in the room,' Andy explained.

Believe me, Andy's *not* the type to imagine anything that's not there, so I was pretty astounded by this statement. To this day he insists it was my dad's voice that he heard, which was quite deep and had a very distinct tone.

When I'm reading for people I 'hear' the spirit person pretty clearly, but I very rarely hear 'outside' my head. It's happened on two occasions, but as a rule, it's an extremely rare phenomenon. About ten of my clients have told me that they've experienced it though, and now Andy was privileged enough to be amongst this elite set of people.

One evening, Helen asked me if Andy and I would like to go on holiday to Cyprus and Egypt with her and Roger.

We hadn't had a holiday since our disastrous honeymoon to the Lake District, where Andy had been laid up all week with a really bad tummy bug. Helen had managed to find a really great deal, so we said we'd be delighted to go with them.

When I was about twenty-two, I'd had a reading at a massive holistic festival in London. The reader, a lady in her fifties with the highest hair-do I'd ever seen (think Marge Simpson), told me I would be going to Egypt at some point, and it would be an incredibly spiritual experience for me. So far, nine or so years later, it hadn't happened, but her words had always stuck with me. She had told me that on seeing the pyramids it would trigger an intense memory of a past-life lived there over three thousand years ago.

Now, out the blue, the opportunity to go to this far away, mystical place had presented itself to me. And who was I to fight fate? (Plus, I wanted to work on my tan!)

The Cyprus bit was very nice, but it was the couple of days in Egypt that I was really desperate to get to.

The big day finally arrived. We all poured off the ship, the usual array of tourists, complete with sun-hats and cameras.

After a couple of hours coach trip to Giza, we finally arrived at one of the seven wonders of the ancient world – The Great Pyramids!

I felt about as excited as a chimpanzee who'd been given unlimited access to the banana section at *Tesco's*!

Impatiently I waited for the tour guide to finish her speech over the microphone, letting us know what time we needed to be back, and warning us about the Egyptian peddlers. Apparently, it was free to get on one of their camels, but costs to get off!

I stumbled off the coach, almost falling down the steps I was so busy gawking at the unbelievable majestic structures looming in front of me.

This was it! This was where my memory would be triggered and past life images would flood through me.

It was going to be sooo incredible.

Like a powerful magnetic force was pulling me along, I glided in a dream-like state towards the three ginormous pyramids, Andy towing behind, snapping away with our newly purchased camera. Before I reached my destination, an Egyptian man intercepted me, interrupting my long-awaited appointment with my past self.

He was clutching a stripped red and white cloth, which he plonked on top of my head without warning.

'Take photo, plise,' he commanded Andy.

As I linked arms with the gentleman, Andy happily snapped away. Then I handed him back his props and we started to walk away.

'Now, money, plise,' the man said.

Oh, right! I didn't realise he would want paying, but I suppose it was fair enough. Andy sorted him out while I had my eyes set determinedly back on my goal – the largest pyramid.

Trying to manoeuvre my way through the swarms of Egyptian men, chattering away as they tried to show me their various wares, I gestured over at Andy, so they would pester him instead.

The pyramid was now metres away. I knew that if I could just touch one of the stones then my promised 'profound spiritual experience' would begin.

Finally, my sweaty palms rested on the surprisingly cold but smooth stone block at the base of the great pyramid. I shut my eyes in anticipation.

Nothing!

No images. No flashes of long-forgotten memories of an ancient life lived!

What was going on? Ever since I'd found out we were going to Egypt I'd been building up to this moment. Now we were here, absolutely nothing.

Zilch!

Looking back, I'm not quite sure why I put so much store on this particular prediction. Usually I'm very sceptic about this sort of thing. But the reader had been so *sure*. I suppose I *wanted* it to be true.

The rest of the day passed in a blur. I didn't take much notice of the no-nosed Sphinx, or the various sights and sounds around me.

Back at the ship, I lay in my bunk and thought about my disappointing day. Helen, Roger and Andy had spent the evening discussing the amazing time they'd had. I'd listened, nodding and smiling at the appropriate places, but I felt so cheated. It seems so silly now, but at the time that's how I felt.

When we got home, I sat down with a cuppa to look at the photos. As I flicked through them it suddenly dawned on me that I'd spent so much time and energy on waiting for this amazing *inner* past-life experience to happen, I'd totally and utterly *forgotten* to enjoy the *outer* experience of being in that wonderful place at that *precise* moment in time. What a waste!

How many of us forget to *really* enjoy living in the moment because we're so busy brooding about the past and lost experiences or opportunities, or worrying needlessly (most of the time) about future events?

Talking about the future, I wanted to say a little bit here about 'predictions'.

There are basically two main theories on this incredibly tricky subject. They are:

1. Everything in our life is pre-ordained. Before we're born it was all planned out, and there is hardly, if any, room for manoeuvre.

2. We have complete free will and are totally in control of our own lives and destinies whilst on Earth.

I personally believe that when we 'pop out' we have certain missions to complete, and things we would really like to experience or learn, but sometimes things don't always go to plan.

It's like going on holiday and having an itinerary, but if you choose not to follow it too closely, that's cool.

Your tour guide might encourage you to visit certain places, or experience certain things, but that's up to the individual.

One of my pet hates is when someone calls me and asks; 'Are you the fortune-teller?'

Being a medium is about giving evidence that a deceased person is alive and well in the next realm of life. It has very little to do with telling the future, although, like other mediums, I'm often asked to pick up future events for people.

There *are* times when of course our loved-ones or guides *will* reveal aspects of possible futures for us. Spirit will always try their hardest to steer us in the direction which is the most beneficial for us.

Our guides and loved-ones have access to a much larger picture than *we* have, so are in a position to give us future insight and guidance on our lives.

It's a bit like meteorologists that predict the weather; it's not that they are randomly guessing. They are using the technology available to them to what boils down to 'predicting the future'.

Our guides are also much more in tune with the universal laws of cause and effect, and therefore their advice can be invaluable to us.

Quite a good example of this was a reading I did for a young lady called Mandy, who I saw at a private house in Surrey a few years ago.

Mandy had two office-job offers, and was looking for guidance to what was the better option. I advised her to take the second job, which she was quite doubtful about.

About a year later I saw her again, and she told me she'd taken the job I'd suggested, but had left after a few months as she hadn't enjoyed it very much, and had had some major problems with her new boss.

I felt really guilty and embarrassed I'd been so far off the mark with my advice.

When I joked that I was quite surprised she'd wanted to see me again, she explained she'd given me the benefit of the doubt because I'd had linked really well with her grandparents. This installed in me that I'm a medium *not* a future-teller!

But as we got to the area of relationships (another tricky area) all was revealed to me. She had met her current partner at this short-lived job, and they were getting on fantastically. In fact, I was pretty sure a wedding could be on the cards! I pointed out that that was obviously the REAL reason she'd been guided to that particular job. I suppose she could've met someone equally as nice as her partner at the other job, but that we'll never know.

Strangely, Mandy hadn't made the connection. When I pointed it out she seemed quite shocked. Spirit must've known this guy would be at that place and would be perfect for her.

It reminded me of the time I'd been told NOT to do the aloe vera business, which had been correct, it *was* a disaster, but it'd been a *crucial* stepping-stone to other, more important, opportunities.

Sometimes I'm asked silly things regarding the future, such as; 'Where should I go on holiday this year?'

I just answer; 'Where do you *want* to go?'

I wanted to share with you a rather strange experience I had just after we got back from our Egypt trip.

It happened in the village hall at Bisley, a venue we'd done a couple of times in the past.

The hall always seemed to have a slight whiff of pongy feet and overcooked cabbage circulating around it for some reason or other – which doesn't relate in the least to the story I'm about to tell you!

The fair started, as usual, at 6pm. I was reading away quite happily, and had done three readings when around eight-thirty I nipped out to the loo. I knew I had another two people waiting for me on my list, so came back as soon as possible. When I sat down and glanced at my little clock (I don't wear watches, never have) it was just after nine-thirty!

I was utterly confused. How could I have been over an hour in the flipping loos, even if I had stopped to run a comb through my hair? I thought my clock was wrong, but no, the main clock on the wall also agreed that it was just after nine-thirty!

I remember feeling so incredibly puzzled. Nothing like this had ever happened before.

I called for the next person on my list but they'd disappeared, probably in a huff that I'd been so long. The last person was still there though, waiting patiently for me. So I put my confusion aside, thinking I'd probably just lost track of time, and did the reading.

When I was packing up my table, Helen drifted over. She looked a little perplexed.

'I'm not quite sure what happened tonight, but I really lost track of time. I somehow lost about an hour when I was reading.'

I couldn't believe what I was hearing. I'd not said a word, not one word. I hadn't spoken to her all evening.

I told her about my experience, and although we can't be a hundred-per-cent on this, it seemed she lost her hour around the same time I lost mine.

I don't think anyone else lost time that evening, although we only mentioned it to Mystic Baz and Roger. Mystic Baz helpfully suggested that we might've been victims to an alien abduction, and very kindly offered to hypnotise us, which we politely declined! Somehow (can't think why) alien beings hiding out in Bisley village hall toilets, waiting to abduct a couple of psychics, didn't quite ring true!

About three months later when we were back at the same place, I did mention my time-loss experience to a lady and her daughter. To my astonishment I was told that other people had had similar experiences in the hall. I can't verify whether this is true or not, but I don't know why they would just make it up.

I'm still hoping that one day I might find out about our lost hour, but as the time slips by, it's looking unlikely. If anyone out there has had anything similar happen please let me know.

One day, Andy and I arrived at a fair in Horley. Huffing and puffing as I lugged in my suitcase, I was very surprised to see hardly anyone there, even though it was quite late.

'Where is everyone today?' I asked Helen as I passed her table.

Helen looked suspiciously red-eyed. 'Cindy, Margaret,

Martin and some of the others have started up their own fairs. They've nicked a load of Roger and Baz's venues and have just gone off. Apparently they've been approaching our readers for weeks and asking them to work for them instead.'

Cindy ran the crystal stall, and Martin was the husband of a tarot reader called Margaret. The thing about a psychic fair is that it *has* to have one major stall, or it can't really charge an entry fee. No one wants to pay £2.50 to enter a fair that only has readers there and no stalls to look at, so the crystal stall is crucial. They are also very hard to come by, so losing Cindy would be quite a blow. It takes so much work to unload all the merchandise and set it all up, then pack it all up again at the end. Because of this not many people are willing to take it on. It's a pretty big job just setting up a reader's table, let alone a large crystal stall!

I glanced over at Roger, who was making his usual cup of tea. His usually pleasant face was like thunder – which wasn't surprising given the news.

I was shocked. 'My God, Helen, that's terrible.'

Helen nodded, lowering her voice. 'Poor Roger's devastated. He's worked so hard building up the fairs. They were *supposed* to be our *mates*.'

I glanced over at Roger who was now sitting at Baz's table, clutching his mug. They were deeply engrossed in conversation.

As I went across to start to set up my table, Roger called me over to them.

'Anne, did Cindy ask you to read at the fairs they're starting?'

I shook my head. 'No, she didn't.'

I could feel the blood rushing to my face as I spoke. I felt (and probably looked) guilty, even though I hadn't done anything wrong. It reminded me a bit of the time I was called in front of the Headmaster when I was nine for playing up in class.

People were starting to arrive at the fair. I saw that Andy was manning the door, something Martin usually did.

'Roger, *everyone* knows Helen and I are best mates. Cindy would know Andy and I wouldn't do that to you. We didn't know a thing about it. Honestly.'

Roger nodded, obviously satisfied that I wasn't part of the mutineer-brigade.

My stomach was a gurgling tight bundle of nerves as I rushed back to my table. I had a few readings already booked in, and my first client had arrived bang on opening time – eleven o' clock. She was sitting patiently, waiting for me.

Flustered and upset, I really struggled at first to click into spiritual mode. The low energy and negativity emanating round the hotel room was almost tangible. As there were only a few of us reading, we were kept pretty busy all day long. I've always tried to take as long as needed when it comes to my readings, and I wasn't about to rush just because I had lots of people on my waiting list. I methodically made my way through my list, given each person a good forty minutes of so. In the end some got tired of waiting and went off.

As one lady commented to me that day; 'When you're waiting for your reading you're thinking 'hurry up, for goodness sake', but when it's your turn you're thinking, 'Don't you dare rush me'!'

Roger and Baz soon found another crystal stall ran by a really lovely lady called Sue, a tiny lady in her fifties with long auburn hair and a wonderful sense of humour. Sue was a very kind lady, but had quite a fiery temper.

In the future something would happen to me that would make me deeply regret the day Sue joined our fairs, but at the time I welcomed her and the other new readers into our midst. Harmony was restored; for the time being, at any rate!

Although all the internal politics that went on at the fairs was sometimes very depressing, the people I read for more than made up for it.

I'll never forget a very smartly dressed gentleman who asked me to read for him at a fair in Dulwich. He eased himself down into the seat, giving me a cheeky wink.

'I'm ninety-four, you know, dear,' he grinned, showing off a pair of gnashers just a bit too perfect to be real.

'Really? You don't look it,' I said politely. It was the truth. He didn't look a day over eighty!

I explained what I did, expected him to want me to link with his loved ones. Actually, I was really looking forward to getting stuck in. At his age I should think that there would be a queue down the hall, out the door and halfway round the block!

'No, no, no, dear,' he told me. 'I don't want any of the dead through. I know they're all fine. I just want my future.'

He chuckled, obviously amused at the look of surprise on my face.

It turned out to be a fantastic read. I picked up on a lady called Ivy, which he told me was his new girlfriend. He was really worried that she was too young for him, as she was only (in his words) a snip of a girl at seventy! In fact, his daughter was *older* than Ivy, and that was what was concerning him the most. I told him to just relax and enjoy this new wonderful relationship that had entered his life so unexpectedly. There *was* an appearance from three or four of his family members, and he was very happy to accept their evidence and messages that Ivy was really good for him. It taught me that it doesn't matter *how* old you are, there are still new experiences, fun and joy to be found.

Bring it on...

Talking of age, going from one extreme to another, I was at a very quiet fair at Tring rugby club one evening, when I was aware of a load of giggles and exuberant shouts from the doorway. The room was long and narrow and my table was positioned closest to the entrance.

Various heads kept popping round the door, then disappearing, accompanied by bursts of hysterical laughter.

'Go on, ask her!' I could hear someone saying. Three young lads suddenly trooped into the fair, nudging and whispering to each other.

They only looked about fourteen or fifteen, and judging by their clothes, had obviously just finished their rugby training.

'Excuse me, can my mate have a quick word with you?' one of the lads asked, pushing his reluctant friend towards my table.

'Of course. Take a seat,' I smiled, although I was feeling a bit worried that I was about to get the mickey taken out of me Big Time!

The young guy plonked himself down while his mates wandered off to look at the crystal stall.

'I was just curious about all this spooky weird stuff,' he told me sheepishly. 'I mean, come on, there's gotta be more than this world, hasn't there? When my granddad snuffed it last year, we had loada weird stuff happen at our house for weeks after. Could that have been him?' he shrugged, looking expectantly at me.

I nodded. 'It's possible. The people we lose are always trying to let us know they're still about.'

This young lad then proceeded to fire at me a stream of intelligent, well thought out questions, which covered everything from religion, the nature and meaning of existence, and how and why loved ones attempt to communicate through mediums or other methods, such as dreams. He even mentioned animals and insects, wondering where they fitted in the great scheme of things.

He'd clearly given it all a great deal of thought, and he totally blew me away with his deep philosophical questioning.

He listened intently as I did my utmost to answer him as fully as my understanding and experience allowed. Finally, his mates stomped over, grumbling at him that we'd been ages, and that they wanted to go for their long awaited McDonald's.

I was quite astonished to see that over half an hour had passed since he'd sat down. I was quite disappointed he was going as it'd been one of the most stimulating and deeply interesting conversations I'd had in yonks.

Another conversation I had with two ladies at a fair in Aldershot wasn't quite as pleasant, but was just as memorable.

I could sense the animosity radiating from these two ladies as they menacingly approached my table, with an obvious mission in mind.

'Excuse me, love, but what makes *you* so f***ing special that you can talk to the dead, and *we* can't?'

'You're just conning people, go on admit it!' the second lady hissed at me. 'It's all a load of bull!'

I tried my best to assure them that I certainly have *never* for one moment thought I was better than anyone else just because I was a medium.

As for conning people, yes, mediums are often accused of that, and maybe a very few individuals *are* motivated by material gain. But I most certainly wasn't.

I don't want to have to defend or justify the relatively small amount I charge for a reading. All I can say is, the time I was at the fairs I would've earned more per hour with a cleaning job, and would've had a great deal less stress to deal with!

There was many a time I attended a fair and broke even after all my expenses were paid, or actually *lost* money. This wasn't a one off event. It happened on quite a regular basis. On Sundays there was always a little more opportunity to earn, as it was a longer day, but I could never rush through them, and rarely did more than five or six. I don't want to come across as hard-done-by. I was doing what I *wanted* and *needed* to do, and that counted for a hell of a lot.

I felt quite shaken up by this unexpected confrontation by these two extremely verbal ladies. I'm not sure why they made a bee-line for me, but I dealt with the situation as best I could, grateful when they'd *finally* vented their anger to their hearts content, and fumed off, leaving me in peace. Phew!

8

Learning Many Lessons!

All mediums will have certain readings tucked away in the back of their minds that stick with them forever.

There are quite a few I vividly remember, but one extremely harrowing reading I experienced was at a Sunday fair in Newbury.

The fair had just opened when a man around his late thirties asked me if I would read for him. His eyes were red-rimmed and he looked incredibly troubled.

He told me he wanted a link with Spirit. I explained I would do my best, but it couldn't always be guaranteed. He said he had some photos if it would help. Did I want to see them?

I declined. People often ask me about photos, but I've never liked working this way. If the spirit person is really there, then they will pass on evidence in their own way. The couple of times I have linked with photographs, I admit that they influenced me in such a way that my subconscious kicked in and took over, which is *not* good!

In some respects, mediumship is a race between spirit's mind and the medium's mind, especially in the early days of development. If a spirit person is not truly present, then the medium's mind will willingly step in to provide the information instead, without the medium realising this. I've seen this happen many, many times when I've been on development courses. It's very difficult to tell the difference and only time and practise can eradicate this common problem.

Within minutes, I had a young lady step forward. I knew it was his wife. I described her, which is pretty standard stuff, and gave her age of passing. Then she showed me something very unusual. I had a clear image of a river. I realised then that she'd drowned. He understood this, but blurted out he couldn't understand how or why it'd happened! She'd only gone for a walk by the river near their home. How did she end up drowning? He told me he suspected that she'd been murdered, but I honestly didn't feel this was the case.

This was so difficult because it would be arrogant and dangerous to *insist* that she hadn't been murdered. I *could* be wrong. This lovely lady was only thirty-two years old, same as me at that time, and she gave me a *lot* of specific names, dates, and memory links with her husband to back me up that what had happened was some sort of freak accident, and not, as he believed, foul-play.

I could only tell him what she was telling me. I was with him almost two hours, and he said I'd helped him more than I could ever realise, but I wasn't so sure. What if she *had* been murdered and I'd told him it was an accident?

After the reading I had to get up and do a demonstration, but it wasn't my finest hour as my mind was going over and over the reading. A little voice was driving me crazy, whispering I could've been mistaken in what I'd told him.

By the end of the day I'd totally and utterly convinced myself that I'd got it all completely wrong – the poor woman *had* been murdered, and I'd convinced her husband that it'd been an accident!

This reading haunted my thoughts for many months. But finally I realised I'd done my very best for this unfortunate man and his wife, and managed to let it go.

I've always had this habit of going over what I've told people and checking I haven't done any damage with my words. It's my biggest fear. Being a reader is such a major responsibility. People are putting great trust and faith in your words, and it's a massive privilege to be part of their and their loved ones' lives for that time they spend with you.

Mediumship is all about getting the right balance. There's no point being so worried about giving the wrong evidence or life-advice that you constantly 'play it safe' and sit on the psychic fence I've seen this with some readers, and the result is wishy-washy, ambiguous advice that their sitters could get off any newspaper horoscope page.

On the other hand, the reader *has* to accept that the information coming through *could* possibly be flawed. This can happen for a number of reasons, but the main reason, in my experience, is that normally the *interpretation* of the information is at fault.

One tarot reader at the fairs could often be heard proclaiming in an arrogant tone throughout her readings; '*I know I'm right!*'

Maybe she was. Maybe she wasn't. The point is mediumship and any psychic work is *not* an exact science. The medium can only do their best to keep the evidence and messages as unpolluted by their own mind and thoughts as possible.

Occasionally bogus-evidence will creep in, like weeds will inevitably appear in even the best kept gardens. To ignore or pretend this doesn't ever happen is equivalent to sticking your head in the sand. Once I was able to admit to myself that my mind *was* interfering with the true evidence I was receiving from the spirit person, I was then able to 'catch myself' when doing this. Now, although it still happens from time to time, it's much less frequent.

Most of my clients are really interested in mediumship and how it works, and often ask how spirit people give me their evidence and messages of survival.

I know from my conversations with other mediums that we all work in our own individual way, but most of us use what's commonly referred to as 'The Three Claires'.

Clairvoyance, Clairaudience and Clairsentience, which basically means, clear-seeing, clear-hearing and clear-feeling. There is also what I call, Claire-knowing. You just *know* certain information. Usually within a reading I'll be aware that a combination of all the Claires are being used to some degree.

Mediumship is something that isn't static. All mediums, whether they are just starting out or are world-famous and on the telly, are learning and growing in their knowledge, abilities and understanding of the spirit world and its people, all the time. (Well, hopefully *most* are!) It's such a vast subject, and just as you think you've cracked it, something will come along and show you that in reality we all know so little about how it all really works.

So far, I've only mentioned mental mediumship, but there's a whole branch of mediumship, which deals with physical phenomena. In recent years I've become a little involved in this particular area, and I'll talk about that in more detail a bit later on.

Contrary to what the sceptics think, there isn't anything more annoying to a medium than someone who comes for a sitting, plonks themselves down, then proceeds to give you their or their loved-one's life-story before you've even offered them a cup of tea.

When I first started as a professional reading, I found it *very* hard to be assertive, and when someone was in full flow I found it almost impossible to shut them up!

But if a reading is to be successful the medium *has* to take control, and very politely but firmly ask the sitter not to say too much. It's the *reader's* job of providing the evidence, *not* the sitter.

In my early days I tried to rectify this problem by telling my clients to say as little as possible, or even better not a word. The result was the poor things were so worried about putting their foot in it that they just sat and stared at me totally dumb-struck.

At first I thought it was absolutely wonderful. Ha, just me jabbering on about their lives and loved-ones, and, yes, when I asked them at the end they seemed to understand what'd been said, but something was missing. The readings felt very cold and impersonal. Yes the evidence was there, but still, I could see people were not as happy as when I'd let the reading proceed naturally.

So I went back to my old system, but with a difference. As soon as someone started to give too much away I would jump in and stop them. I didn't sit back and politely wait for them to finish.

Once a link has been established and evidence has been given, I think it's only natural and very healing for the sitter to want to talk a little about their loved-one's, or the problems on their mind.

I've never trained to be a counsellor, but anyone with an ounce of compassion in their soul can see the healing that takes place when someone expresses their innermost feelings about the loss of a loved one, or a split from a partner, or a problem with a child. The list of course is endless. As a reader it's important to get the balance right. Most of the time this will happen naturally, but there will always be those times when you need to take control of the reading.

I only wish I'd taken this advice with a reading that I did around four years ago, for a gentleman in his sixties.

Right at the beginning of the reading he told me that he desperately wanted ONE specific piece of evidence. If I gave him it then he would believe one-hundred-per-cent.

I listened, a squeamish sensation building up in my tummy. Ahh, there's nothing like good old pressure!

Linking fairly quickly with his wife, she gave me some very nice pieces of evidence. Each time I told him something, he seemed to feel the need to talk for ages, going through all the details I was passing him. As a rule I don't like this, as I want spirit to provide me with the information, not the client. But as he was clearly choked up with emotion, I let him talk. As he chatted, his wife clearly showed me a white dove. Not wanted to interrupt him in full flow, I thought to myself; *I'll tell him about that when he's finished talking*.

He was recalling a very interesting dream he'd had, and I became so engrossed I *totally* forgot about the dove. I count this as the biggest mistake and regret I've ever had in my career as a medium.

Overall, he thought the reading was very good, but admitted he was bitterly disappointed I hadn't come up with the prime piece of evidence he'd asked his wife to pass to me.

I listened in horror as he told me why he was desperate for me to mention a *dove*! The story behind the dove and its significance is quite long and personal to him so I won't go into it, but the dove was most definitely important.

The tears were streaming down my face. He patted my hand, thinking I was moved by the dove-story, which I was. But in truth I was crying because I was so totally mortified that his wife had given me this crucial piece of evidence, and I'd let them both down by not passing it on. It would've meant the world to him.

I couldn't help myself from telling him that I *had* seen the dove, but the moment was gone. There was no way I could prove it. I sent him a card in way of apologising for my mistake, and he's seen me for a couple more readings since then.

I learnt a lot the day I made that mistake with Dove-man, as I call him. If someone starts talking too much, I gently and quickly try and shut them up!

On the subject of birds and animals, a common question people ask me is whether our pets also go to the spiritual realms when they pass on. Of course the answer is *yes*.

I'm sure there are many books dedicated to the Animal-Kingdom and what happens to their souls, so I won't rabbit on about that. (Sorry, that joke was groan-worthy!)

In my career as a medium, I've linked with many pets,

and it's a wonderful experience to feel the *intense* love they have for their human friends.

There are two animals that I will always remember.

The first was the most beautiful horse that linked with me a few years ago. The lady I was reading for, Dana, understood a horse in spirit and also took the description and name I gave her. Then I had a vivid picture of her plaiting the horse's mane, using loads of coloured ribbons. I don't know a great deal about horses, but I don't think this is a very common thing to do. She couldn't stop laughing when I mentioned that Joe the horse told me he didn't really like the 'hairstyles' she used to insist on giving him.

A week or so later and I received an e-mail from Australia, where Dana was living. It was of Joe, complete with colourful ribbons and plaits, which looked very pretty indeed.

Another lady I read for about a year ago, had a lovely German Shepherd come bounding up to her in her spirit-form. This beautiful dog gave me some very specific information about herself, including her passing date.

I didn't get the dog's name, as the lady had blurted it out in excitement when I'd first made the link. (I don't know if I would've got the name or not, but I would've had a flipping good try, as pet's names are fantastic evidence!)

A few days later, I was in bed, opened my eyes, and there was the German Shepherd staring down at me. I could only really see her head and shoulders, but what surprised me was that she was surrounded in red roses. I knew straight away that it was the dog I'd linked with earlier that week, as the dog had been called Rosie.

Another reading I did that has always stayed with me is a couple who I saw at a psychic fair in Bexley. I linked with their toddler son, who'd passed over in tragic circumstances. He gave me his name, Joshua, and some other specifics, which were confirmed. What was so memorable about this reading, was the courage and strength of this young couple. Their absolute resolve to get out there and continue living life to the fullest. As Joshua's mother told me; she wanted to try and experience everything on their son's behalf.

Joshua was so very proud of his parents for having this attitude. It's incredibly hard for spirit people to watch their loved-ones suffering so much over their loss that they can hardly function on a day-to-day basis any more.

I remember one lady who'd lost her son in an accident telling me that if she did anything remotely nice she felt like she was somehow being disloyal to him. But in truth, whenever she *did* have a good day where something positive happened, he was as pleased as punch for her.

It's so hard as bereavement hits people in so many different complex ways, and not everyone can find the strength to go on and be happy once again. My one wish would be for people to see how their loved-ones are truly safe and well, and immensely enjoying the next phase in their new life.

At the same fair that I'd read for Joshua's parents, I had a very attractive lady in her thirties approach me for a sitting.

It turned out to be more of a life reading that she wanted rather than mediumship, and overall it was going fairly well, until the lady suddenly burst into loud sobs. I couldn't quite understand what was wrong, as we hadn't covered anything *that* emotional, and from what I could tell the lady had a fantastic life – loving husband, a beautiful teenage daughter. Also, she didn't need to work to earn a crust as her husband ran a successful business.

I didn't seem to be picking up on the problem like I normally do, so I had to resort to asking her what was up.

Her reply was surprising. She confided in me that her husband had cut back her allowance, and she now couldn't afford to go on a girlie holiday her friends were arranging. It was causing a real strain on their relationship.

I felt her husband was a generous man, and couldn't

understand why he would begrudge her a week with the girls. She then explained to me that she had already had two holidays that year, one with him and one with her daughter, but felt she deserved a third one.

As I took in her expensive clothes and nail extensions, I realised that this lady was just a spoilt pampered-princess. And she was sitting there expecting me to be sympathetic towards her as her hubby was being so 'unreasonable'.

I politely suggested that it might be quite a good idea to get a part-time job and save for the holiday. (I was rewarded with quite a nasty look for that particular comment!)

After the reading I went and had a cup of tea and sat outside in the hotel lobby, marvelling about the differences between Joshua's parent's reading and the one I'd just done.

I always try to help people to the best of my ability, but the last lady had really tested my patience.

I had a bit of a moan to my team upstairs about how 'some people don't know they're born', expecting them to sympathise and agree with me, but I was in for a bit of a shock.

I heard these words spoken in my head:

'You can't judge or compare one person's needs to another's. The lady who just consulted you was, from her perspective, being treated unfairly. Whether that's the case or not isn't the issue. She came to you for help and advice.'

'Which I *gave* her!' I replied indignantly.

'Yes, but was it done with non-judgemental love?'

When I thought about it, I did feel rather guilty. My reading *had* been tinged with scorn towards her, and, if I'm honest, a fair bit of envy thrown in that she had it so cushy. But I still thought my guides were being a bit harsh with me that day – after all, I *am* only human! It's not easy feeling love and light towards everyone all the time!

An evening I'll always remember was a charity-ball Helen, Roger and I were invited to read at. This event was at Goodwood House, near Chichester, which is connected with the famous Goodwood Racecourse.

We arrived early to set up our tables. The idea was the guests were to have a dinner and dance, and if they wished they could come along and have a mini-reading for twenty pounds with one of us. All the money we took would go to charity.

I watched enviously as the ladies arrived in their stunning, glittering evening gowns, and pretty high-heeled sandals, their hair all piled elegantly on top of their heads. The men looked great as well in their tuxedos. I couldn't help wishing that I was a guest, and not here just to read. I half wondered if it would be possible to trade in my guide for a fairy-godmother instead. Much more fun! Maybe Honrad could get himself a pair of wings, a tiara and a nice swishy wand! (Then again, on second thoughts, maybe not!)

Oh well, by this point I was pretty much used to not having much of a social life, as many of the fairs were at the weekend, and going out in the week isn't really the same. Most of my mates had totally given up asking me out on Friday and Saturday evenings, as they knew I always liked to get an early night if I was reading the next day.

The first hour was pretty quiet, as the guests were having their meal. But soon enough the odd guest or two had the confidence, fuelled I'm sure by the flowing champagne, to venture bravely into our separate room.

'What's all this about then?' inquired a gentleman, clutching his glass of champers.

'We're doing psychic readings tonight, all for charity of course,' Roger explained. 'Do you want to give it a go?'

The man laughed. 'Go on, then, why not?'

I expected him to sit at Roger's table, but he plonked himself down at mine instead.

'Do you want my palm to read, or what?' he asked, thrusting his shovel-like hand at me.

'No, that's okay, thanks,' I smiled politely as I silently

asked my team to draw close. The only thing I was concerned about was that we were under instructions not to take too long over the readings, as the aim was to earn as much as possible for the charity.

The shortest reading I'd done was about half-an-hour, and even that was unusual. Usually a reading lasted at least forty minutes. I find there is always so much to cover when reading for someone, and I like to do a thorough job. I wondered how much could be picked up in just ten or fifteen minutes!

This gentleman had obviously had a very full life judging by the information that flowed through me straightaway. There was *so* much to pick up on I had to speak at a speed that made my voice raise a couple of octaves. I ended up sounding like I'd swallowed a bucket of helium!

I can't remember very much of what I told this guy, but I *do* remember that he kept asking me how I knew certain things about him. It was quite funny really. He'd obviously never had any sort of contact with the paranormal in any shape before this experience. I do remember giving him both his son's names (I've always been pretty good with names) and that's when he insisted that I must've had a chat with his wife, who was also at the Ball. I didn't have a clue who his wife was!

Later in the evening he dragged her in, and I ended up reading for her as well. In total, I think I did about seven or eight mini-reads. I was shocked at how much relevant and specific information could be picked up in such a short amount of time. Roger and Helen also did really well, so between us we raised a very nice amount for the charity. I actually got a good few recommendations from this lovely couple, and some of the others I'd read for, so I did quite well out of the evening.

Another time I had to 'condense' my readings was at a singleton's night in Bracknell. I had a phone call from a lady organising the event at a hotel, asking me if I would like to pop along and do some readings for the singletons.

I said yes, I would love to, thinking it sounded like good fun. I assumed they would all want to find out about their future love lives!

It turned out I had to read at a psychic fair that day, as one of the readers had let Roger down at the last minute and I said I would step in. The fair at Guildford finished at 7pm. It was quite a busy day, so by the time I got to Bracknell, just after eight, I was pretty knackered.

A very well-spoken gentleman showed me to a cute little office. To my delight it had cute jars of sweets dotted around the room, which would go down well, as I hadn't had time to eat. I also had my own kettle to make hot drinks.

After a cup of Earl Grey (my fave) and a good few handfuls of very nice mints and boiled sweets, I felt revived enough to start the evening.

I even had my own day-glow orange poster on the door. It read: ANNE, PSYCHIC CLAIRVOYANT.

Blimey, my very own poster! I was going up in the world!

I was kept very busy with a steady stream of singletons all evening. Funnily enough, contrary to my pre-conceived ideas of what they'd want to know about, none of them seemed that particular interested in hearing about relationships. All sorts of stuff seemed to be coming out though. I even picked up with one very sceptic guy that he was off to India later that week. He almost fell off his chair with shock. (I love it when that happens!)

An added flattering bonus was that I had two guys asking me out on a date, which, of course, I politely declined. (I didn't mention this to Andy, who was patiently waiting for me to finish in the reception area.)

Finally, thank God, the end was in sight... It was about two in the morning when I got to stagger to the car, supported by Andy, for the drive back to Bognor. On the way back as I drifted into sleep, I swore to myself that from now on I would stick to one commitment per day!

Another time we were at the same hotel in Bracknell, doing a psychic fair, I popped out to use the bathroom. Opening the door of the Ladies, the smell immediately invaded my nostrils. The whole place was full of dense, grey smoke.

I covered my mouth and ran inside to check out that no one was in any of the cubicles. I was worried they might've been overcome by the smoke. Thankfully, the place was empty. Most of the smoke seemed to be pouring out of the small bin in the end cubicle.

I rushed to reception and informed them of the situation, then went back to my table.

One of the staff came over to thank me for my swift action and told me that the smoke detector seemed to be faulty. The source of the smoke had come from someone having a crafty cigarette in the cubical and sticking it in the sanitary-towel bin without distinguishing it properly.

Not too clever! The idiot could've burnt the whole flipping place down.

The problem was I now stunk strongly of smoke. Nice!

My third reading after this event, a lady sat down at my table who wanted me to link with Spirit. Her dad came through and gave me some good pieces of evidence to pass on. I noticed as I was working that the lady kept looking about and sniffing the air. I guessed she could smell the overpowering stink of smoke on me, and was embarrassed she might think I was a chain-smoker.

At the end she told me she often smelt cigarette smoke when her dad's spirit was about, as he'd always been a heavy smoker, and she'd smelt it strongly during her reading with me.

Red faced, I had to explain that although the spirit person often *do* create smells associated with them to grab our attention, on this occasion she wasn't smelling her dad – it was definitely me!

In the spring of 2002 I experienced one of the very best and incredible weeks of my life.

Helen and Roger had attended a residential course at a place in Essex, and had returned raving on and on about how absolutely incredible it'd been, and what an amazing place it was.

Helen insisted that I just *had* to go, but the trouble was I didn't have the confidence to go on my own, so I nagged poor Andy until finally he agreed to come with me just to shut me up. Whilst I was there I kept a detailed diary of events, and thought it would be a good idea to present them to you in this way:

Sunday March 31st

What a place! The energy here is incredible. Soon as we arrived we went for welcome tea and coffee in the dining room. Everyone seems really smiley and friendly, but they all seem to know each other. I'm glad I've got Andy. I'm feeling annoyed at myself for not talking to the lady who grinned at me at tea-time. Andy's eyes nearly popped out of their sockets when he saw the deserts on offer here. He's in Cheesecake-Heaven. I knew I should've packed my spot-cream as I'm going to break out big time after the chicken pie and chips and huge bowl of trifle I scoffed down.

Went for a chat with my tutors. They seem really nice. Told them I see spirit people, and hear them, etc. Andy had a go at me because I didn't tell them that I'm a professional reader. I don't think they're really that keen on psychic fair's here from what Helen told me. They want to put me in the advanced group. I'm not sure if I'm up to that. I bet they're all fantastic platform mediums!

Just got back from the evening of clairvoyance service. It was okay, but nothing mind-blowing. Found the mediumship a bit wishy-washy. I thought they were going to be amazing. Andy didn't enjoy it much.

Have got a bad headache. Going to get an early night. This room we're in is supposed to be most haunted bedroom in the building. I so love the four-poster. Andy's grumbling as it's a little lumpy! (My side is fine. Ha, ha.) Wonder if I will see anything tonight.

Monday, April 1st.

Didn't see anything, but Andy said he saw loads of orbs in the night. He's really excited, as he's never seen anything before.

Just had our first class. We're in the library, which is the home to thousands of ancient-looking books. Going to ask if I can borrow a couple of them. We just chatted about what we've done in our development so far, etc. Bit boring. Hope we get to work soon, I'm itching to get going. Lady in my group called Val gave me some headache tablets. Feeling a lot better now.

Andy said his group was really good. They had to take a psychic 'peek' round their partner's house. Told me he picked up quite well.

I'm still a bit shaky. Had to stand up in front of the group and link with someone in spirit. It felt a lot harder than at the fairs. Having the tutor breathing down my neck made me really nervous. I linked in with a guy in my class called Jack. His cousin, who died in a car accident, stepped forward. Was quite good stuff, but felt really uncomfortable with everyone watching. A lot of the others are training to be platform mediums. Val and Jack were really good, also a girl called Whelma from Denmark. The others were a bit weird with their evidence and messages. Jack told me I work very naturally. Not quite sure what that means, but I think it was a compliment!

This afternoon was great fun. We had a class with the guy tutor. We had to partner someone and draw round their hand. I was spare, so I had to team up with the tutor! I drew round his hand and then sketched little pictures that related to him and his life. He showed mine to whole class and explained how it was relevant to him. I'd drawn scales of justice, and he said he had a legal matter going on at the moment. He understood all the little names and other things I had drawn. Even the blue rose! (Hope he wasn't just being kind.) He did my hand-picture, which was a bit weird. It was depicting a nursery rhyme, which I didn't quite get! (Oh, God, maybe he was picking up a pregnancy!)

Just got back from the bar. Had a few wines and a good old natter with quite a few people. Feeling really relaxed now. Can't wait for tomorrow.

Tuesday, 2nd April.

The tutor wrote the name of a spirit lady on the board and we had to write as much as possible about her. I was worried how she would link with all of us at same time, but the tutor assured us that it wouldn't be a problem. I just wrote loads of information down. It was pouring out like water from a tap. It's really good to just link with spirit without the pressure of someone sitting expectantly opposite you. When we'd finished the tutor told us the lady was her mum. When the tutor came to me and I read my notes she said; 'Now, *that's* my mum!' It was a really fantastic exercise. I did pick up one thing a little incorrectly. I got the name Sam and thought it was a dog. It was the spirit ladies grandson!

Had a lovely walk round the gardens after lunch. The weather's pretty good today. It's so peaceful here. Something a bit weird happened in the shop. A load of angel cards flew off the shelf in front of me and landed extremely neatly in rows on the floor! Andy said 'clumsy', but I didn't flipping touch them. I bet this place is full to bursting with mischievous spirits all having a great time playing tricks on unsuspecting students.

A guy in my group called Paul keeps saying he senses great sadness with me. I know it's been stressful the last few years, but I wish he would stop saying it. It's starting to get on my nerves. He wants me to give him a reading tomorrow after lunch. I really don't want to do it!

Really, really tired. Bit low and teary this evening. People have been so kind and said some lovely things to me today, so I don't know why I feel so upset. It's strange but this place seems to dig deep right into your very soul and drag out every single emotion, good and bad, that's trying to hide inside you. Can't wait for my personal reading in the morning.

Wednesday, 3rd April

Just came back from my personal reading and I'm a bit disappointed. Dad came through. Well – I *think* it was him. A couple of bits were relevant, but there wasn't anything really specific. No names, dates, or memory links. She did get he passed over with cancer, but that was about it. I was shocked when she told me I could possibly be a professional reader in a few years' time if I got myself in a development circle. I've been a reader for over three years now and doing quite nicely, thank you! Andy was annoyed and said I should've told her, but I felt too embarrassed.

To be fair, she looked really tired. Jack said they overdo things here, and should probably just stick to teaching rather than trying to do readings on top of everything else.

Oh my God! We had to pair off this afternoon and give each other a reading. My partner was the young Danish girl, Whelma. She totally blew my mind with the evidence she came out with. Dad came through with so much evidence. It was like he was trying to make up for this morning. He mentioned June, his sister, and gave me our wedding anniversary. She got his character and description exactly, but I couldn't believe it when she said Dad was telling her about the operation I'd had when I was twenty, and about me very nearly dying. No one knows about that, and it was one of the last things Dad mentioned to me before he passed over. Whelma also said Dad was showing her a mirror, at which point I knew without a doubt it *was* Dad!

Dad teased me constantly because I spent my life as a teenager staring in the mirror. In my defence, eighties-style hair and make-up did take at least four hours to apply! When he passed over, we found a load of cartoons he'd doodled of each member of the family. Mine was a caricature of me staring in a mirror with a thought bubble: 'Ohhh, aren't I beautiful!'

I could really feel Dad standing there working with this young girl. I told her it was the best reading I'd ever had, but I think she thought I was being kind. The reading I gave her went really well too, but I think her one was amazing. She doesn't even do it professionally – she's a teacher at a kindergarten.

This evening I had a long chat with Whelma. She wants me to go over to Denmark to stay with her and read for her friends and family.

Thursday 4th April

This morning I sat under the huge ancient oak tree to do my 'homework'. I linked in with a lady and scribbled down all the information pouring into my mind. It was extremely interesting to just go with the flow and jot it all down without having a sitter to interrupt or influence me in any way. It felt amazing. Just me, the spirit lady, and my notepad! I sat for around fifteen or so minutes, and in that time ended up with a page full of scribbled notes. I've got to read them out later today. God, I hope they make sense to someone!!

After lunch I read my notes out. Everyone (about eight in total) had to stand up and listen, then sit down when the information no longer applied to them.

This is a list of my notes:

1. I've a short, cuddly lady with me who passed with heart problems. She's telling me she's an aunt connected to Mum's side.

(Everyone but two people sat down.)

2. This lady had quite a few children, about five, and she's mentioning an Olive or Oliver and James.

(Everyone was now sitting down *apart* from an older lady in the group called Pat.)

Pat told me she felt sure it was her mum's sister, who was one of five and had two sons, Oliver and James.

3. She's mentioning the month May.

Pat shrugged and said it could be right. The tutor asked me what date in May, but I couldn't get a date, and didn't want to just guess. Pat's face suddenly lit up. 'It's her name!' she said. 'She *is* May. Auntie May!'

I *distinctly* remember getting the word *May* in my mind, and assumed it was the month. I will remember this mistake and store it for future reference.

4. I also felt she linked with an Alison on earth. Could be a granddaughter. (Pat couldn't take this but later did tell me there was an Alice, who was a granddaughter, in the family.)

5. She's showing me a rosary. There's strong Catholic links with her.

Pat nodded.

6. She's telling me the person she links with is holding a dinner-party this weekend, and as she's going to be there in spirit, helping to supervise the cooking.

Pat laughed and told me she was having a huge do on Sunday with all the family, and she's doing all the cooking.

I had a few other bits scribbled down about Auntie May, but the tutor said time was getting on. At tea-break Pat accepted the last few loose ends, and thanked me for getting her lovely aunt through for her. She told me that Auntie May was like her second mum. I'm feeling quite pleased with this link, but still feel I held a load back because of my nerves in front of an audience. It has amazed me how much can be obtained without the recipient being present.

I can't wait for this evening. The guy tutor is going to do a trance mediumship demonstration. I've only seen Pete do this before. Apparently this guy's really fantastic.

I can't believe what I've just witnessed!!!

There was about fifteen of us in the library, sitting in a large semi-circle around the guy tutor. I was directly opposite him, so had a good view. The two lady tutors sat either side of him. The lighting was on low, but I could still see clearly.

This was completely different to Pete's trance demo that I witnessed three years ago.

As I stared at the tutor, I noticed a really strong-featured oriental face forming. It looked like a mask that'd gently been placed just on top of the tutor's face. I thought I was imagining it, but I could hear muted and amazed murmurs circling the room. Val nudged my arm and asked me if I could see the Chinese man slowly forming.

I was too shocked to reply. Yes, I've seen loads of stuff, but that's on my *own. Everyone* was seeing this. I must admit, I'm still half-wondering if it's possible that we all had some sort of mass hallucination.

The words spoken from this spiritual visitor were full of love, wisdom and compassion. These emotions were actually tangible, and as he spoke I felt tears streaming down my face. I think a few of the others were also crying, but can't be sure as I was too wrapped up in the experience.

What he said made so much sense to me, on a personal and a wider level. He spoke of the path we each choose, and the individual journey we are all on. That we need to help rather than hinder each other. In short, all the stuff I normally can't stand, as it's all so cliché and flowery. But somehow this was different; so stunningly clear and wonderful. I'm *really frustrated* writing this because I'm not doing the words the guide spoke any justice *whatsoever*. I'm a medium, not particularly educated in the art of words, but I'm doing my best, and that's all I can do!

Apart from his eyes bulging ever so slightly, Andy didn't say much when I told him. (I'm sure he thinks I'm exaggerating.)

I'll need a double whiskey and ginger tonight in the bar! Maybe even two!

Friday 5th April

Just got back from the last class. Mostly chatting about the week and what we've gained. I feel I've learnt so much this week. In all honesty, it's not so much about my mediumship, although I feel more confident in the information I'm getting. It's more on a personal level. I've learnt to be much more relaxed around people. It's okay to give my opinion about things, even if I think people won't agree with me. They *are* interested in what I have to say. It's time to open my mouth a bit more and speak up, rather than hiding in the shadows all the time.

Going down to lunch. It's fish and chips today. Then it's back to the Real World! I'm not looking forward to saying goodbye to everyone. Especially Val, Jack and Whelma. I feel like I've known them for years. I've got my hanky at the ready – just in case!

I'm under the oak tree scribbling this. Thank you my spirit friends for being with me on this incredible week. I pray I can come back here one day very soon.

Two years later I did return, with a dear friend that I was just about to meet!

9

The Attack

I first met Caroline when she turned up at a psychic fair in Bracknell. I was sitting at my table chatting to Helen, when I first noticed this tall, blonde lady in her late-forties with beautiful, startling-blue eyes. I didn't go over and say hello straight away, as she looked a little flustered setting up her table for the first time. She was sitting directly opposite me, and Andy had the table next to her. I watched as Andy handed her one of our spare lamps as she set up.

That particular fair was always very busy, and this Sunday wasn't any different. So apart from a quick hello and goodbye at the end of the fair, we didn't get a chance to talk properly.

Over the next few months we chatted on quite a superficial level, but even so, I could tell that Caroline was a deeply spiritual lady, and a talented psychic and tarot reader who truly cared about her clients. She also had such a wonderful sense of humour, and her laughter always lifted the energy of the fairs.

In the summer, one of the new readers, Donna, held a barbecue at her home, and we were all delighted to be invited along. It was one of the most fun days I can honestly ever remember having. Everyone was in such high spirits. (Well, we were a bunch of mediums after all, so we *should* be in high spirits! Sorry, I couldn't resist that one!)

I spent a lot of the day chatting to Caroline, and we got to know each other a lot better. It was her birthday that week and we had a real giggle at Mystic Baz's present; a book about Tantric Sex! I'll never forget Caroline's face as she ripped off the paper and saw what was inside!

As the blistering hot day turned to dusk, we sat in the garden, sipping chilled wine and playing silly word games, mostly led by Mystic Baz and Ken, a guy who helped at the fairs, usually running the aura camera. This evening stands out so clearly in my mind. Looking back, it was the last time we were all together, relaxed and joking about.

In many respects we truly were like one big family. Yes, we had our fair share of petty disagreements, but on the whole, considering how different we all were, we got on well most of the time. It's wonderful and of course very comforting to be around people who hold similar beliefs to yourself, especially when they differ quite a bit from the majority of people.

A couple of weekends after this memorable day, we were driving to a fair in Bournemouth when I started to feel unwell, suffering with a pounding headache and a horrible giddy sensation, like I'd just got off a roundabout.

When we arrived I had a quiet word with Roger. He sympathised with me and suggested that instead of reading, which takes a lot of energy and is hard to do when you're in full health – let alone feeling rough as sandpaper, that I could run the aura camera instead. It suited him because he didn't have anyone to do it that day, and he would've had to read for people, and also run the camera, which would've been difficult.

I thought this was a great idea, and although I'm not too good with technology, Roger showed me how to do it. Luckily it was fairly straightforward. I was quite looking forward to seeing what auras were going to be captured on film. I would also have to give a very short reading interpreting the various shapes and colours surrounding each person. I knew what the colours meant, but would also tap into my psychic abilities to help me in this quest.

When Andy and I were still doing the aloe vera stall, we'd both had an aura photo taken. Andy's aura was a pale green, which represents calmness and healing energies, and mine was a bright pillar-box red! To me, red usually means stress and worry, but also high nervous energy – which just about sums me up! To be honest, I take aura photos and the colours they produce with a pinch of salt, and see it as interesting and fun rather than taking it too seriously. I most definitely see colours around people when I'm reading for them, which I call their 'aura' but don't usually go too much into the colours and their meaning as there's no real way of proving it, and I'm big on proof, or a reading doesn't mean very much.

How accurate these special aura cameras are, I can't say for sure, but nevertheless, it's *extremely* fascinating to see the differences in each person's unique picture.

It was a very slow start, but around an hour or so later I had my first customer of the day, a bubbly lady in her twenties.

The aura reading went well, and I really enjoyed interpreting her photo. It was quite a nice change to have something tangible to work with rather than having to rely on my psychic and mediumship abilities. As the afternoon crept on, I took a couple more photos, but the day was pretty sleepy. Half the readers looked as if they were about to drop off.

Sue, the lady who ran the crystal stall, had brought her son Lee in that day. He often came along with her and helped out in some way. Lee was a well-built lad of about nineteen or twenty, and seemed like a really nice guy. Everyone liked his cheeky sense of humour. I felt sorry for him as he'd been involved in a horrific road accident a few years back and as a result had been left disabled, and had some degree of brain-damage. I was unsure of the exact nature of his injuries, but I knew he struggled with his walking and co-ordination.

I'd been sitting directly behind him, as he was manning the door, and we'd been chatting and joking together all day. When he asked me to help him get to the bathroom as he was struggling with his legs, I said yes, of course I would help him.

As I helped him into the hotel's disabled toilet, he slammed the door and locked it, trapping me inside with him. At first I laughed and told him to stop mucking about. He told me that he only wanted to talk. From smiling and joking just seconds before, he suddenly turned extremely agitated and upset. I've never witnessed such a quick change in moods with someone before.

What he poured out to me was terribly heart-breaking to hear, and I did my best to comfort him. It all seemed a little surreal, sitting on a disabled loo's floor, having this disturbing conversation with a tearful teenager.

Maybe I was a little bit *too* friendly and comforting because suddenly a huge arm was placed threateningly around my neck, and a hand was thrust down my top. Lee grabbed violently at my breast. I battled with him, trying to pull away his hand, telling him to stop being stupid, trying to play it down. But in truth I was utterly terrified, realising that the state Lee was in *anything* could happen. How on earth had I got myself in this horrifying predicament? After a time, I managed to calm Lee down by reminding him I was a friend of his mum's, and that she wouldn't be too pleased about his behaviour towards me! He was extremely apologetic, and obviously embarrassed about what he'd done.

Finally, outside that horrible toilet, I watched as he limped back to the room the psychic fair was in. He'd asked me not to say anything, and I'd agreed that I wouldn't, but of course I knew I couldn't just brush it under the carpet. It was too serious. What if he gave a repeat performance on a member of the public and I hadn't spoken up? It didn't bear thinking about!

I sat down in the lobby, trying to make some kind of sense of the last quarter of an hour or so.

After a while Roger wandered by, probably off to order

some tea. I called him over and told him what'd happened.

I could tell he was shocked and was obviously very concerned about me. He went off to fetch Andy, as I told him I wouldn't go back into the fair. I just wanted to get home as soon as possible.

Lee's mum came out to see me, wondering what was going on. Roger must've said something. I briefly told her what had occurred, and she promised to speak to him. It was left at that.

Andy was obviously horrified when I explained why we'd had to leave before the end of the fair. I felt really sorry for him – he looked so strained and tense as we drove home, mostly in silence.

Psychic I may be, but I couldn't possibly have known that that day's events would eventually have quite a few repercussions in my life, some good, and some bad.

That evening, I spent quite a while on the phone to Helen, and she was really upset for me. The following day Roger, Helen and Baz came over to our house to discuss the situation.

All I can remember about this meeting is being reassured that Lee would not be allowed, in *any circumstances*, to attend the fairs again. He didn't go very often in any case, but now he was banned forever.

I was so relieved to hear this. I didn't feel any great anger towards Lee, more sympathy. I honestly think that he just got carried away in the emotion of the moment.

But on a personal level, there was no way I could face him again. I just couldn't.

When I told a couple of my spiritual friends what had occurred with Lee, they kept repeating that everything happens for a reason, and suggested that maybe I should meditate on why this had happened to me.

So I did. I lit a couple of candles, sat cross-legged on the end of my bed, and asked for clarity on this particular experience.

Why had this happened?

What *lessons* did I need to learn here?

At first, nothing. Then, slowly, words were forming in my mind. To this day I'm unsure of their *exact* source. But they made sense to me, so I wrote them down:

Your soul comes down accepting that this world can be, and occasionally is, a dangerous place. To your soul, this is actually part of the attraction of an Earthly life.

The soul craves the highs it achieves and feels by overcoming the lows of a physical life. It's like someone who will climb a mountain, even though they know it can be dangerous. The soul enjoys the challenge and likes to test itself – sometimes to the limit. Some souls who choose not to experience physical life call you, who deliberately encase their souls in heavy physical matter, 'The Brave Ones'!

People have free will, and because of this incredible gift, good and bad things will happen. Rather than think something has happened for a particular reason, think about what you can take and learn from the experience to help you become a stronger, better more compassionate person.

I suppose it's only natural that when unpleasant things happen we try and comfort ourselves with 'Oh, that was meant to have happened anyway'. I don't believe that this is always the case. It takes away our personal responsibility. Being brutally honest here, if someone smokes for years and ends up with lung disease as a result, you can't turn round and say, 'Oh it would have happened anyway. It was just meant to be'. That, in my opinion, is crazy.

I know a lot of people, including most of my friends, have differing views on this deep, age-old question, but before you throw this book down in utter disgust, I wholeheartedly agree that many events most definitely do happen for a reason. Quite often when I link with a person that has been involved in some sort of 'accident' they explain to me that 'it was their time'. So, as usual with this philosophical stuff, the answers are not always as straight forward as it seems.

The trick is, when something bad happens to us we should try and seek a way to take something positive from that particular experience.

A couple of weeks after this meditation regarding Lee, Andy and I were driving behind a camper van. It proudly displayed a bumper sticker, which declared so eloquently: *Shit Happens!* Crude, I know, but I think sums it all up rather accurately really!

When Caroline heard about Lee assaulting me, she immediately phoned and kindly offered to come over and give me some healing. She also said that if I needed to talk, she was there for me. I was really thankful for her support, love and friendship. People can be capable of such kindness. I wonder how they would express that generosity of Spirit if nothing bad ever happened? (Another deep question to ponder.)

Our friendship really took off from this point, and it was the one truly good and wonderful thing that came out of all the unpleasantness.

The fairs carried on in relative peace for the next couple of months or so, which, looking back, was the calm before the storm...

I can still recall the moment I felt my body jolt in shock as I spotted the hunched up figure of Lee as he helped set out his mum's stall. It was at quite a large fair near Guildford.

What's he doing here? I thought frantically. I had to get away. Fast!

Roger followed me out of the hotel room into the lobby.

'Anne,' he called after me. 'We need to chat.'

I promise you, I'm not usually a Drama-Queen, I'm mostly a fairly quiet, private person. But to say I wasn't a happy bunny at that particular moment would be putting it mildly.

I listened agitated, the blood pounding in my ears, as Roger explained that Lee's mum had brought him along without warning, and there wasn't much he could do about it.

What? He ran the fairs for goodness sake!

'I can't work in the same room as him, Roger. Sorry, but I just can't!'

Roger shrugged, looking really uncomfortable. 'We *have* to have a stall today, and Sue's threatened she'll go home if Lee can't stay. We had this out with her this morning when they turned up.'

My logical brain could see what an awkward position Roger and Baz were in, but I felt betrayed somehow. I thought they would stand by me on this. They had made me a *promise*. Now Lee was back, and I guessed that if they didn't make a stand now, Lee would be back for good.

'Maybe you'd better leave today,' Roger said quietly.

I had three or four clients already booked in that day, so before we drove home I had to ring around and cancel them, as I didn't want them to have a wasted trip.

The night I had a chat with Honrad, and it really helped me to make an important decision.

I already had quite a few private clients. Many were now coming back regularly (twice a year) to see me. Also, every day new people were calling wanting to book me for psychic parties, but I wasn't sure if it would be sustainable.

I know the money side of things is always a bit of a sensitive subject when it comes to spiritual work, but the reality is I had made this my career, and like it or not, I couldn't live on 'spiritual love and light' alone! If ever I'm fortunate enough to win the lottery I would, without a doubt, give away my services for free. (From my Barbados villa!) But until that happy event occurs, I *have* to charge.

When you have to book in at least seven or eight new readings each and every week just to have a bare minimum of an income – I was charging £25 per private read – and there's no security blanket of the fairs to fall back on, it's quite scary. But scary or not, it was time to move on.

10

Denmark Debut?

After we left the fairs, Andy started a part-time job at a decorating centre near Chichester, so financially things were a little easier.

I was getting quite a few calls for psychic parties, but didn't know if the phone would *keep* ringing. So many of the readers break away from the fairs to try on their own, only to re-appear on the circuit a few months later. But after all that'd happened I didn't have any choice. I *had* to make it work. I'd worked so incredibly hard on fine-tuning my psychic abilities, not to mention my personal skills in dealing with different types of people. As hard and nerve-wracking as it was being a reader, there was *no way* I could give it up now. But it all depended on the phone going constantly.

I needn't have worried. Almost as soon as I'd left the fairs plenty of people seemed to want me to visit them and their friends at their homes. Within a few weeks I was booked up for three months in advance. I would only do about two or three parties a week, as I was still struggling big time with health problems, and found the readings very tiring and draining.

Around this time quite an amazing coincidence occurred when I went to read for a lady called Jan, who also lived in Bognor.

The reading was good, nothing too taxing as all-in-all Jan had a nice life and was quite happy. Her dad made an appearance, giving me his name and the usual kind of information to identify himself. Then he started to chat about his beloved rosebushes, commenting they'd not been pruned right. I'm not a great fan on garden-related evidence, but it seemed to be this gentleman's favourite topic of conversation, so of course I had to repeat what I was hearing.

Jan understood that her dad had been a keen gardener, and had planted some rosebushes he was proud of in their garden, but she didn't understand the bit about that they'd not been pruned correctly.

As I was leaving, Jan asked me if I had far to go. I mentioned where I lived, and she told me she'd grown up in my road. Astonishingly, it turned out she'd lived in my *actual* house – her parents had owned it for quite a number of years. Jan told me that her dad had planted three rosebushes in our garden, and he'd been very proud of them.

I suddenly remembered Andy had been pruning our rosebushes over the weekend, and he'd been a little too enthusiastic with the secateurs!

I'd even had a moan at him about how awful the poor things were now looking, and he'd had to ring his mum, who's an ardent gardener, for advice.

Jan's dad had been grumbling to *me personally* about his beloved rosebushes!

Whoops!

Luckily we got some expert advice soon after that, and they're now back to their former glory.

A little after this reading with Jan, I was faced with a very strange scenario at one of my psychic parties.

I had seen two of the four people I was scheduled to see that day, and so far it was going very well. Then my day went down hill rapidly; the third lady walked in, looking deadly serious, a bundle clutched in her hand.

Before I'd even had the chance to say 'hello, nice to meet you,' the mysterious bundle was thrust at me. Surprised, I took it. It was a collection of photos showing a youngish dark-haired gentleman. I was unsure of his nationality. Studying the pictures, it was obvious the man in them didn't realise he was being photographed as they'd all been taken from a distance.

'Did that man murder my father?' the lady blurted out angrily. 'Tell me now, is *he* the murderer?'

I felt utterly horrified.

I was sitting here in someone's tiny third bedroom, surrounded by a large collection of cuddly toys and spooky-eyed porcelain dolls, being asked to identify a murderer just by using my psychic ability.

Truly scary stuff!

'I'm so sorry, I can't answer that for you.'

'Why not?' demanded the lady. 'Get my father through and ask him. You *are* psychic aren't you? Look at the photos. What do you sense? You must be able to tell me something if you're *really* psychic!'

I knew she kind of had a point, but somehow I felt I was being challenged a little unfairly.

I stared at the photos, trying my very best, but no information came to me. I couldn't see anything, or hear any voices. I couldn't even feel her father in the room. Even if there *had* been anything coming through to me I wasn't sure I could start accusing some guy of murder just by looking at his photo.

Suddenly, I did hear a voice; '*Do not attempt to help in this matter. It's out of your hands.*'

'There must be something you can tell me about this man,' I begged silently.

But no, nothing came. I had to admit defeat as I handed the photos back to the seething lady. She kept giving me these looks as if to say, 'How dare you call yourself a psychic!'

'You came very highly recommended,' she said very quietly, her face shiny red with disappointment.

I then realised I must've been this poor woman's last hope. But there truly was nothing I could do for her. Even if I'd said he *was* the man who'd taken her father's life it would hardly have stood up in a court of law! If she wanted closure I couldn't give it to her.

I can't tell you how truly awful I felt about not being able to help her. It was such a hard lesson to learn – that I have limits, and can't always help everyone. Sometimes we can't see what's going on behind the scenes, and have to trust our spirit friends when they ask us to leave well alone on certain things.

One day a very good friend of mine, Kate, who was a tarot reader that I'd met at the fairs, rang me up and invited me to travel to Denmark with her.

Kate told me she'd been in contact with some TV producers over there who were very interested in meeting British mediums with a view to filming them work and making some sort of documentary. She'd had a preliminary meeting with them and apparently that had gone really well. I wasn't sure of the exact nature of what they were after, but it sounded like too good an opportunity to miss out on! Kate had been on a few psychic-based TV shows, and seemed to know how these types of things worked, whereas I was totally clueless!

Wanting to look my best for the cameras I had my hair done, treated myself to a couple of new outfits, and told all my friends I was off to be on Danish telly!

We booked a couple of cheap flights, and Andy found us an apartment on the Internet. Everything was set for my TV debut!

As I felt the plane lift off the runway, it suddenly dawned on me what I'd let myself in for.

Oh my good God!

I had let Kate's enthusiasm carry me away. My stomach started churning at the thought of having to 'perform' in front of a production team, no doubt reading for a Danish person. Kate seemed laid back and relaxed, laughing and joking with the cabin crew, but I sat rigid, staring out the window. *How* did I manage to get myself in these situations?

But what if I didn't take the opportunity and hid for the rest of my life – always wondering what might have been?

I've always fled away from new experiences, and it hadn't done me any favours. Surely it was better to have a go and fail rather than let my old mate *fear* win again? And maybe I *wouldn't* fail. My spirit friends had never let me down. In the four years I'd worked with them – apart from the lady whose father had been murdered – there had only been one time that I hadn't been able to link.

This had been at a fair at a hotel in Horley. As I sat there on the plane, sipping my orange juice, it was this one reading that my mind kept churning over, not the hundreds of successful ones I'd done.

I can sum up my first impression of Denmark in one word, well, maybe two – *Bloody Freezing*! To be fair it *was* January. Maybe not the most sensible time to visit a Scandinavian country. In places the snow was almost up to my knees – I'm only short! For some strange reason I'd forgotten to pack my snow-boots, skis and husky dogs! Very remiss of me!

But in compensation for the weather, the apartment was very nice, apart from one teensy-weensy problem – it only had one bedroom, and worse still, *one* double bed! The lady who owned the apartment hadn't mentioned this fact, thinking a married couple had booked the apartment.

As much as I was fond of Kate, I didn't really fancy sharing a bed with her, but what else could we do?

After the initial embarrassed giggling and silly comments had subsided, we both then proceeded to experience the most restless, disturbed sleep we'd had in years.

'Are you asleep, Anne?' Kate whispered to me, sometime during the early hours. 'Can you *feel* anyone here?'

'I'm not sure,' I whispered back.

There *was* a really creepy feeling in the apartment, but it wasn't anything I could put my finger on. Yes, I work as a medium, but that doesn't mean to say I can link in with every stray spirit person within a ten-mile radius. And anyway, normally I feel uplifted if a spirit person is present, not creeped out!

'I can sense a lady watching us!' Kate suddenly blurted. 'You *must* be able to feel her, Anne. Surely?'

'No, not really,' I admitted. Kate was a very good medium, and I had the highest respect for her ability. If she could feel a lady, then I believed her.

In the morning, we both pottered bleary-eyed about the apartment, getting showered and breakfast, not talking too much. We were both pretty knackered after our restless night.

As I nibbled unenthusiastically on my toast, my stomach was in great knots. The last thing on earth I felt like doing was trying to impress some hot-shot TV people. Walking over a shattered crystal ball in bare feet seemed more appealing at that moment!

But after the war-paint had done its faithful job, we both perked up a bit.

Kate had been a little sketchy on the finer details of the meeting. But as it all seemed under control, I hadn't really questioned her too much about it. The plan seemed to be to make our way into town, and then give some guy a call. He would then pick us up and take us to meet the rest of the team, to discuss exactly what they wanted us to do.

Well – that *was* the plan...

When Kate attempted to call the guy he basically refused to talk to her, let alone see us! To this day I have no idea why.

So, there we were, sitting in a Danish café, done up to the nines, freezing to the core, our glittering TV career in tatters before it'd even begun!

Looking back, it was quite amusing really, and we probably should've had a good laugh about it and just enjoyed the break. But the build-up of anticipation, then the big let-down, not to mention the bitter cold and lack of sleep, had all taken its toll!

We started bickering. Kate thought that we should just jump on the next plane home, but I wanted to say a couple of days, as the apartment was booked, and try and get something out of the wasted trip. In the end I agreed with Kate, as I wasn't staying there on my own, and we decided to leave the following morning.

Back at the apartment, Kate started picking up on the spirit lady again.

'She killed herself, and I'm sure she's trapped here,' she declared, as we munched our takeaway pizza. 'She needs our help to move on. Maybe that's the *real* reason why we had to come here.'

I was dubious, still unable to feel any mysterious lady. But what if Kate was right? I hated the thought of some poor woman floating about aimlessly in the ether, trapped in-between the two worlds.

We sent prayers and pleas for help out to her, and soon Kate said she could feel a strong shift in energy, and felt the lady had finally been able to 'move on'.

This whole 'stuck spirit' thing has always confused me because I can't believe that anyone who passes over would be left by the spirit community in such a miserable state of existence.

It goes against everything I've experienced and learnt about the next world. I decided that the next chance I got I would have a little chat with my guides and get their opinion on this subject.

When I'd been younger I'd always been secretly terrified that when it was my turn to meet Mr G Reaper, I would end up lost in the Mists of Time, trapped, lonely, for all eternity in some dreary location. Not a pleasant thought!

Relaxing on the flight home, I shut my eyes and started chatting to Honrad and the gang, asking them the questions on my mind. Sometimes I wonder if they get sick of my endless stream of queries. I hope not! I don't want to give the false impression that every single question I put to them is answered straight away, because that's just not the case. Often, the answers I want come to me in rather a strange way.

I could be having a casual conversation with someone, or reading a particular book, and suddenly the answer to the question I'd asked days previously is there, staring me in the face.

But occasionally, as soon as I ask a question words pour into my mind. On that flight home my guides were obviously in a chatty mood because as soon as I asked them about trapped souls, words started to flow:

'Not one soul is ever left behind!

It cannot happen.

Those of our world would not allow it.

There are always a tiny number of souls who, for their own personal reasons, refuse to leave your world after their passing. As they have the right to exercise their freewill, this decision will always be respected. Even so, it is almost always for only a short amount of time. When they are ready we gently encourage them to make the crossing to our side of life.'

Honrad then added in a rather humorous tone; '*We have had quite a bit of time to practise helping souls cross over, you know!*'

I asked about the lady who Kate felt had committed suicide, but didn't get an answer one way or the other if she really existed. Oh well, we'd done our best to help her out.

My next question was a personal one – I had a bit of a bone to pick with My Lot! Why hadn't they warned me that this trip would be a total waste of time, energy and money? Three things I was desperately short of.

As I reclined in my airline chair to await the answer, I could've sworn I heard a gentle chuckle:

'We wouldn't dream of stopping you from having this or any other experience. Sometimes more is leant when things don't go quite to plan than when they do? Why would we want to interfere with this natural process?

Your soul has asked to go through many types of experiences whilst it's on its Earthly journey – some joyful, some frustrating.

Of course, we will always try and give you our advice and support when we feel it's really needed, but we think you'll find you have gained more than you have lost by this particular trip.'

The only thing I seemed to have gained is flipping frostbite! I thought grumpily, as I scribbled down the words I was hearing, hoping to mull them over when I wasn't so tired.

A while after my Danish experience, I received an e-mail from a lady representing a charity for people with sight problems. She wanted to know if I would spend a night in a local 'haunted hotel'. Around ten people would be sponsored to spend the night in a room that apparently had had a lot of psychic activity reported by guests. I would be the medium for the evening, seeing what information I could pick up.

It didn't take my arm twisting to say, 'Yes, I would be delighted to offer my mediumistic ability for the night'. I hadn't really done anything like this before, and couldn't wait to see what would happen. I expected at least half a dozen previous residence of the hotel queuing up, wanting a natter with me. I'd taken on board what Honrad had told me about there being no 'lost souls', but surely in a five-hundred-year-old hotel there would be a few floating about, wouldn't there?

11

Where Are All The Ghosts?

The big night arrived. Armed with little more than our toothbrushes for the morning – and my makeup bag, of course – Andy and I drove over to the hotel.

It was a truly impressive building, sporting the black beams against the whitewash background, in keeping with the Tudor era it belonged to.

Inside were the standard low-beamed ceilings. Ha – I knew being quite short would come in handy one day!

We followed a member of staff through a labyrinth of narrow stairways, and twisty, turny corridors, finally arriving at the 'haunted suite'.

Dramatically, he stopped at the door, a mournfully expression on his face. 'Sorry, but this is as far as I will go,' he whispered sinisterly. 'Good luck to you both. See you in the morning.' Then as an afterthought he added, 'Hopefully!'

Charming! I don't think he realised that I was the medium. He probably thought I was one of the sponsored charity-raisers, and he'd been told to 'ham it up'! The young lad was absolutely wasted working here; he should've been an actor!

As it turned out we were the first to have arrived, which gave me time to have a quick nose about the place.

The bedroom was stunning, with its huge four-poster, and lavish furniture and paintings.

'Can we get a bed like that?' I pleaded to Andy. 'And I do love the way they've draped the curtains... '

Andy rolled his eyes. 'You're supposed to be picking up on paranormal activity. Not getting interior design tips.'

'I'm a woman, I can multi-task,' I snapped back.

But in fairness Andy was right. I *should* have been tuning in and seeing who was about.

I sat in the adjoining living area and quietly sent out prayers, asking my team to help me make contact with their world. My nerves were starting to kick in. I knew that very shortly people would be arriving, and as the medium they would be looking at me to 'deliver the goods' for the evening. This was totally different to giving someone a reading, which works on the vibration of need and love. No one here *loved* any of the long dead spirits connected with the hotel. No one really *needed* them. So why would they communicate with us?

I suppose I could link in with the charity-raisers loved-ones, but that wasn't the purpose of the evening.

An hour later, the twelve or so charity-raisers had arrived, clutching their sleeping bags, pillows and blankets. One girl had even brought along her teddy bear! Ahh!

Andy and I hadn't brought any bedding, as we'd thought everyone would be staying up all night – but this lot were obviously planning on getting their beauty sleep.

The very nice lady who I'd arranged the evening with, couldn't make it, and had sent along another lady who made it quite clear that she didn't really believe in any sort of paranormal activity, thank you very much! She promptly plonked herself down on the four-poster, claiming it for the night, and left us all to sort ourselves out.

No one seemed to know what to do, and I wasn't sure of my role, as I hadn't been introduced as the medium. I was feeling so anxious by this point that if Henry VIII himself had appeared in front of me and done a tap dance followed by a rendition of *Greensleeves*, I wouldn't have sensed a flipping thing!

Finally, Andy took the lead and introduced me. Bless him! We then sat cross-legged as he took the group through a guided meditation, while I 'tuned in'.

After the meditation, a very friendly lady who was a journalist for the local paper, started to tell us about the previous month when the charity had ran a similar event at a nearby hotel.

Apparently, the medium had 'seen' a battalion of Roman soldiers marching majestically through the room they'd all been sat in. The medium had also picked up bucketful's of spirits connected with the hotel that were for one reason or another 'unable to move on'. They'd spent half the night rescuing these poor unfortunate souls – and went home feeling quite the Heroes of the Hour, I'm sure!

Sorry to sound a little sarcastic, but as you can guess, I did feel a little dubious about these events being for real.

I could feel myself grinding my teeth as I sat listening. God! How was I going to compete with all that? The group kept glancing at me and asking if I was getting anyone through yet? Help! Yet again my 'hole in the ground' had deserted me when I needed it the most!

Someone suddenly mentioned that a young servant girl had been murdered in the very room we were in around two hundred or so years ago. I was asked if I could link with her. I think they might've been trying to help me out a little, but it just put me under more pressure as the group kept asking me if I could feel her.

I certainly couldn't feel, see or hear her. Thinking about it, why on earth would this poor girl want to return to the place of her gruesome murder? Surely it would be the very *last* place on earth she'd want to be, wouldn't it?

In the end I had no choice but to admit the depressing truth – that I honestly couldn't sense any spirits wanting to make contact with us.

Don't get me wrong. I knew there were plenty of spirit people about, such as guides and relatives, but none that wanted to communicate at that time. I couldn't just summon one up on cue.

I got the impression that these people didn't want a medium – they wanted an entertainer! I felt so awful letting everyone down. To my shame, it did briefly cross my mind to wing it and make something up! After all, the evening *was* about raising money for charity, and was supposed to be a fun event, so it was all in a good cause. But there was no way I could do it. I have too much respect for my spirit team and the work we do to stoop to telling fairy-stories.

Shooting me disappointed glances the group started to climb into their sleeping bags, snuggling down for the night. Knowing everyone was thinking what a crap medium I was, I crept out, red-faced and very dejected, to the adjoining living room.

Andy didn't say anything, but he slipped his arm round me to give me a reassuring hug.

Two of the group – a lady and a younger guy – suddenly appeared, saying they were unable to sleep because of someone's atrocious snoring.

We got chatting and before I knew it I had the young guy's grandmother standing next to me, asking me to pass on some very personal messages and evidence to him.

Two hours and several relatives later, we decided to get some sleep. The guy couldn't stop thanking me. He told me he'd never had a reading before, and would never in a million years have gone for one. He'd been 'dragged' along to this 'ghost-hunt' by his female friend. I was so thankful that something positive had come out of the evening.

In the following months, quite a lot of work materialised for me out of this one off-the-cuff reading.

My work as a medium has taken me to many private houses and buildings, and it always fascinates me how the energy changes in each one.

Some people are just naturally sensitive to energy, and when they enter certain buildings they get 'dark-feelings', or feel 'positive and energised'. It's a fact, in my opinion, that inhabitants of a place will leave their imprint in it, and over time certain emotions will build-up, which can be 'picked-up' by sensitive people. In most cases the majority or buildings will of course be a mixture of many emotions, but in some rare occasions certain places will have a strong build-up of one type of particular emotion. An obvious example is a prison, which will most likely have a large amount of negative, angry-energy swirling round it. On the other hand a church will have a build-up of loving, positive energy. (This isn't always the case, but you get the jest!)

Sometimes, the negative energy in the atmosphere around us can affect the moods of sensitive people – just as dust in the atmosphere can affect people that are sensitive to allergens.

I can remember being invited to a home in Portsmouth to do some readings a couple of years ago. I set off in a relatively happy mood, but once I'd entered this house I was immediately overwhelmed with sadness and just wanted to burst into tears.

The people were really nice and chatty and friendly, and the readings went very well, but all evening I couldn't shake off this intense feeling of sorrow. When I'd finished, the lady of the house confided in me that she thought her home was being haunted by the spirit of a young man. Apparently, he'd taken his own life there ten years previously.

'My friends get the shivers here, and won't stay over,' she explained to me. 'Can you sense the young guy here, Anne?'

I wandered round the house, silently asking him if he wanted to make himself known. But no, nothing.

The words '*He's moved on'*, went through my mind. Suddenly I just knew the dark-energy in the house had been built up by the powerful emotions of his parents. They'd suffered such terrible pain after his death, and because *emotion* is a very real energy, this pain was still being 'felt' by many people.

I told this to my host and she confirmed that the young man's parents had lived there for quite a while after his passing.

'What can we do about it though?' she asked.

Ahh, this was the tricky bit. Although there are various techniques such as smudging and prayers that can shift negative energy, in truth only time can disburse it. Also, creating 'happy-energy' to cancel out the powerful negative ones, would be a good idea. I explained this to my hostess, and she understood there wasn't a quick 'solve-it-now' solution. (There never is!)

She smiled and said she and her partner would just have to make a supreme effort to create new positive, joyful energy. That'd have a lot of fun trying in any case!

One day I had a phone call from Helen telling me she'd just had the most incredible, mind-blowing weekend of her life, attending a self-development course in London. Helen's always *very* enthusiastic about everything, but this time her enthusiasm seemed to have reached new heights. Her excited babble wafted down the line, drawing me in as I listened in amazement. It sounded awesome! After about an hour of chatting, my only question was; 'When's the next course running?'

My next question was; 'How much does it cost?'

I expected that it would be totally out of my price range, but Helen surprised me by saying I could pay whatever I could afford! Some people gave ten quid, others hundreds of pounds. It seemed a little too good to be true, but Helen assured me it was all above-board, and that she thought it would really help me to deal with the terrible anxiety attacks I suffered before my readings.

Deciding it was worth a try, I booked a place for the following month. Arriving at the hotel in London, I really had high hopes that after this course all my problems would magically melt away.

The first thing that I noticed was how well spoken and dressed most of the others were. It soon became apparent that the majority of the people were young professionals who seemed quite stressed out with their high-powered careers.

The first person I had a conversation with at coffee break was a youngish lady who complimented my hair. Then she started moaning about how much money *her* hair cost to maintain every year. A figure was mentioned that was more than half of my annual income with the readings! She told me she was a solicitor, then asked me what I did. I muttered I was a consultant (don't laugh) and quickly changed the subject before I could be questioned to deeply on what people 'consulted' me on!

As I took in her well-tailored designer clothes, immaculate hair and posh accent, I wondered what I was doing here. I thought these would be spiritual people, but it seemed they were professional business types. I was absolutely convinced that I wouldn't have anything in common with this bunch of 'yuppies'. They just weren't my cup of tea! I decided that I would keep myself to myself – and as for telling them what I really did... there was more chance of Andy joining the Royal Ballet! (He would never fit in those tights anyway! Ouch!)

But to my surprise as the day went on and I got to work with the others on the various exercises we were set, I found they were really nice, genuine people. They were just trying to do their utmost to become the best they could be in this muddled world of ours.

Alone in my room that evening, as I reflected on the day, it dawned on me that I'd judged them all on the way they'd spoken and the clothes they were wearing without even *knowing* them. I was a medium for God's sake. I should've known better than to start judging everyone, and straight away putting up my barriers.

The truth was my own insecurities and doubts about myself had made me feel totally inferior to them, with their high-flying careers. I was scared about what they would make of me if I told them I was a medium.

Since I'd started reading I had fibbed, or wasn't entirely straight to certain people, about what I did for a living. I'm ashamed to admit that I felt a certain amount of embarrassment and apprehension in telling people I talked to the dead for a living. (I think there's a pun in there somewhere!)

I always felt so worried about the reaction I would get off people, especially professionals such as doctors. So I chose to bend the truth. I was fearful of being judged as a deluded nut case, or worse, a con-person, praying on the vulnerable and bereaved.

As I perched cross-legged on my hotel bed, I started to get really angry with myself.

What was the worst that could happen if I told the truth? I'm sure no one has ever been killed by a raised eyebrow before! (Not to my knowledge, anyway!)

Many people have their *own* spiritual beliefs, some of which I find bizarre, but I still respect them! So *surely* I was entitled to mine?

I felt so honoured and privileged to be able to help people connect with their loved ones in spirit. It's incredible to witness the inner peace they get from communication. I was extremely proud of being a medium.

Stuff it! Let them think what they liked! From now on I would tell people what I did if they asked.

This was a major decision in my life. It might sound as cheesy as a slab of Stilton, but by deciding to tell people the truth, I felt I had finally accepted *myself*. I had decided to *stop hiding who I truly was*! Oprah would be proud!

When the inevitable chit-chat at coffee break took place the next day, I stood to my decision and said boldly; 'It's a little unusual, but I'm a medium!'

Everyone was incredibly interested. No dirty looks or snide comments. Better still, no killer eyebrows! In fact, most of them wanted to know if I was picking up anything for them.

I explained that I was off-duty this weekend, but they were welcome to call me and book a reading. As the weekend progressed I did end up yielding under pressure and giving a few mini-readings.

Funny thing was, Helen had been right – I *did* get a lot out of this course. But not because of the various exercises we'd done, as interesting as they were, but because I'd learnt not to be so hasty to make a judgement of people just because I didn't think they were 'my type'. And of course because of the decision I'd made, and the relief I felt from simply speaking my truth without being scared of ridicule.

I felt I'd become a stronger person – which was just as well, because if I'd glanced into the crystal ball I would've seen that the next few months were going to be the most difficult of my life.

12

Where Have They Gone?

The night I got home from my course in London, I suffered an extremely nasty asthma attack. As an asthmatic, it's difficult to explain the panicky feeling you experience as the breathing tubes suddenly decide, without warning, they're going to take a nice little holiday from doing their job for a bit!

As I sat on the bed coughing and wheezing, struggling for air, I prayed to my spirit friends to draw as close as possible and help me through the suffering. Immediately I was aware of them, especially Nan, who's always around when I'm very poorly. Although it was comforting, feeling them by my side, I was still gasping for breath.

Of course Andy was with me, doing his best to help the situation. He wanted to call an ambulance but I wouldn't let him. I've always dealt with these attacks on my own, and although this was far worse than anything I'd experienced before, I honestly couldn't bear the thought of being carried off to hospital in an ambulance.

Just as I was about to give in and let him call, my breathing mercifully eased. I must've coughed up at least a couple of pints of thick dark green mucus. Sorry to be so graphic!

The attacks continued to plague me night after hellish night.

I was on very strong antibiotics, but they weren't really doing much to help. Days turned into weeks. I was forced to cancel my readings. After waiting quite a while to see me some people were understandably less than happy, but what could I do? Finances were becoming extremely tight, which wasn't helping my stress levels in the slightest. It was fine for all and sundry to tell me to take it easy and just concentrate on getting better, but I was watching everything I'd built up since leaving the fairs evaporate before my eyes. People were patient up to a point, but I knew many would soon get tired of waiting and consult another medium. At this rate I would have to start over from scratch!

My life reverted to coughing and wheezing most of the night, then sleeping all the following day to allow my body to recover from the assault. Weeks slipped into two months. I was given a bucket load of medication, but just couldn't seem to shake off this stubborn chest infection.

I cried out every night to my spirit mates to send me healing, but I think psychologically I was in such a state I just couldn't feel them around me anymore. I managed to convince myself that they'd totally deserted me when I needed them the most.

Oh, yes, they're always there for my clients but not for me! I thought bitterly.

I felt so angry and, frankly, ready to pack it all in. All the help I had tried my absolute hardest to give to others over the past five years; all the sacrifices I'd made. And in my time of desperate need my team had disappeared off the face of the Spirit World! Where the hell were they – on holiday with my breathing tubes?

This was something I scribbled down during this time:
(*Warning – hankie alert*!)

I do my best to keep going every day,
But I know I'm slowly turning to grey,
Fading like the evening light,
I know I'm gonna have to fight.

I need some help but don't know where to turn.
What lesson here must I learn?
To live, to laugh, to be alive,
For this I must try and strive.

Deep and dark, stuck in this maze,
I'm trying to see through this haze.
Where is the light
That once shone so bright?

At this lowest point in my life I would so much *love* to confess to you that I was visited by a Host of Heavenly Angelic Beings, but unfortunately this didn't happen – well, not that I'm aware of anyway. But after three months or so, I *did* slowly start to recover.

My anger towards my spirit friends began to fade as my negative thinking subsided. In its place were cool rational thoughts. Of *course* my spirit friends hadn't deserted me. It had been my ability to *sense* them that had temporarily disappeared. I felt so totally ashamed of my rants about how they'd let me down. I knew in my heart that they'd helped me as much as possible during my illness.

Whilst I'd been poorly, I'd been informed by one of my clients that spirit people will always sent 'extra special' healing to those who work within the spiritual arena. When I really thought about this, it made me feel very uncomfortable. Why should I have preferential treatment just because I was a medium? Many deserving people suffer from a whole host of medical conditions. I do NOT believe that spirit people would put mediums over anyone else.

On this vast subject of healing, although my experience is quite limited in the area, I wanted to express a few of my views here.

I know many people *receive* healing, but there must be a limit to what Spirit can do, or no one would ever be ill. I don't truly understand why certain people seem to suffer – through no fault of their own – so much. I believe it comes back down to our soul *volunteering* to occupy a human body with all that entails – including illness and pain in all their various forms. The soul realises and accepts physical problems as 'part and parcel' of the Earthly Experience.

Interestingly, after my three months of intense suffering, I noticed that I'd become a much more compassionate and tolerant person. I'd fancied myself as quite a caring person before my illness, but I suddenly noticed that I had tons more sympathy and patience towards anyone suffering in any way. I wonder sometimes how such beautiful qualities such as compassion and empathy would develop in people if no one needed any help in any way!

Andy decided that after the three months I'd been through I really needed a treat. He suggested I book a course at the college in Essex. As he said, it would be the *perfect* way of easing myself back into the psychic world.

As silly as it sounds, I was really nervous about going on my own, and we couldn't afford for both of us to go. As a solution, I had a ring round my mates and Caroline said she'd be delighted to go with me.

We scanned the prospectus and Caroline spotted a Native American course running in September that she really fancied. The same week was a course that really caught my attention. It was titled *Investigations into the Paranormal*. From the write-up, the week would be a real mixed bag with all sorts of experiments taking place. It was exactly what I needed.

I didn't realise that by booking this course I was about to experience my very first amazing taste of *Physical Mediumship*!

13

Entranced!

The first of many surprises I encountered that week was the tiny amount of people on my course – there were only seven of us, all female. The whole college was filled up with the Native American lot, a really friendly vivacious bunch.

The tutor's running my course were a grey-haired lady with a fantastic sense of humour, and a younger lady called Sharon with masses of shiny black hair, lots of bright crimson lipstick, and a really infectious laugh.

The first session was a little different to what I had been expecting. Sharon produced a pack of cards, which she told us were called *Zener* cards. The cards depicted five different symbols – a square, a circle, a cross, a star and a squiggly line.

Groans circulated the room as we guessed what was coming next.

'These cards are seen as kindergarten stuff by the seasoned psychic,' she told us brightly. 'But how many of you have ever tested yourselves by using them?'

She laughed, taking in our blank expressions.

'Okay, so who wants to give them a go?'

'Now don't get too excited, ladies!' the grey-haired tutor joked.

Pieces of paper were duly passed round, and we were told to tick the box corresponding with the card we thought was being held up to us.

Being 'tested' in such a cold, clinical way felt quite a nerve-wracking experience, but I actually got the first card right, which was very encouraging. Then my logical brain kicked in – and it all started to go horribly haywire! I got the next four cards completely wrong.

God, I was *supposed* to be psychic and yet I couldn't even 'tune in' to what card was being held up!

Glancing round, everyone was pulling pained expressions and there was a lot of tutting and low murmurs circulating the room. I comforted myself with the thought that at least I wasn't the *only* one getting it all wrong. My brain desperately tried to figure out what card would be held up next.

My thinking process went something like this:

Well, the star was last, and it was the square before that, so now it'll probably be squiggly's turn. Yes, squiggly's not made an appearance yet!

Somewhere in the deep recesses of my mind I knew I wasn't supposed to be using logic. I was *supposed* to be turning in psychically. But the weird thing was I just couldn't help myself from thinking like this. My need to be right and *prove* to myself that I *was* really psychic was so great it was causing the *exact opposite effect* to take place!

Maybe I'd been kidding myself all these years. I was about as psychic as a teapot! (Even less in fact, as even a teapot can produce tea-leaf readings!)

This course was supposed to be building up my confidence after my illness, not stealing away the little belief I had left in myself.

Then I remembered that I hadn't 'opened up'. I always go through a series of short exercises before I do any sort of psychic work. In my heart I know these exercises don't really make any true difference to the quality of my readings. It's more of a habit I got into when I first started at the fairs. The exercises mentally prepare me, and get me 'fired up and focused' before my readings.

The trouble was I'd trained myself to such an extent that subconsciously my psychic faculties now wouldn't operate until I'd 'opened up'.

Hastily, I ran through my routine in my mind, focusing on the psychic centres, starting at the base of the spine, stomach, heart, throat, up to the top of my head. I'd developed an emergency-opening-up-session, which took about thirty seconds.

Done!

My mind now relaxed and focused, I was relieved to get the next card right, and the next. In fact, I got five in a row correct! Which I was chuffed to bits about. Sharon was very impressed.

At lunch my warm fuzzy-feelings after my morning's performance quickly faded, as there was a bit of a disagreement on our dinner table.

Somehow we'd got on the subject of age. An immaculately presented lady, who I would guess was in her early sixties, announced that no one under the age of forty should be a professional medium.

Her reasoning was that the older you get the wiser you become – and you can't be a medium without wisdom. In addition, you must've suffered 'untold misery and pain' to gain enough 'brownie points' to qualify as a medium.

On top of all that – and she stressed this was *incredibly* important – you should've sat in some sort of development circle for at least three years before attempting any kind of psychic work.

On all counts that ruled me well and truly out!

1. I was under forty – thirty-five to be exact.

2. I wasn't particularly wise and hadn't suffered terrible agonies. Well, not too much compared to others on this planet.

3. My total time of sitting in development circles was approximately two hours – and that was back in 1996!

This lady sounded so very eloquent and educated, and I knew the others were taking her words to heart. A lot of them were nodding enthusiastically and murmuring their agreement.

I'm not a confrontational person, but I couldn't agree to her argument that age brings about wisdom. It *can* be the case that age brings wisdom, of course that's true, but not *always*. And just because someone is young it doesn't exclude them from the wisdom-club.

As for her theory on having to suffer to become a medium, this seems to be a common theme. Again, in my opinion, there is *some* truth in this statement, but suffering is relative, isn't it?

Most people on the face of the planet have suffered to some degree. How much is enough to make a medium? I've met many wonderful mediums who've had relatively happy lives.

Humans are incredibly complicated beings. Tough times can make them emotionally stronger, but it can also just as easily make them weaker. There are no hard and fast rules. Whatever we are, young, middle-aged or getting-on-a- bit, one day we can be wise, strong and compassionate, and another day we can be negative, weak and judgmental and certainly not brimming full of wisdom.

It varies.

As for the age thing, well, all I'm going to say is; if our spirit friends think that I, or anyone under the magic age of forty, am good enough to work with, then how can anyone else put an age limit on it? It's crazy how people pick up these set ideas about things.

Her last argument regarding the development circle also made me feel quite cross. Circles are fantastic for many people, but they are certainly not for everyone. I know, without a doubt, they would've held back my development. I *had* to be thrown in at the deep end. I'm a quiet private person and who've felt intimidated practising my psychic abilities in front of a group. It would've destroyed my confidence. The opposite could be true for many others. We are all individuals and need to find out own way – NOT be told we *have* to do it this way or that way.

I tried my best to put across my feelings and views on these important subjects, but as usual I didn't articulate them very well, and left the table feeling frustrated and angry with myself, as well as Lady Know-It-All.

After lunch, Sharon asked us if we wanted to try our hand at dowsing. Of course we were all eager to give it a go.

An object had been hidden in the college, and we had to wander about, swinging our pendulums in every nook and cranny in the hope of locating it – much to the amusement of the college staff.

I've never been a huge fan of pendulums, and I think the one I'd borrowed sensed my dislike because it seemed to have a flipping life of its own! It just would *not* behave under my control, and couldn't make its mind up to what was 'Yes' and what was 'No'. After half an hour of fruitless random dowsing, I ended up standing at the colleges' aquarium, watching the colourful fish warily eyeing up my erratically swinging pendulum, probably worried it would crack their watery home. Surely they hadn't hidden the object in the fish-tank of all places!

But alas, no, I was completely wrong. My 'trusty' (ha bloody ha) pendulum must've been having a right old chuckle to itself. The object was hidden on the other side of the college, on the mantelpiece by the huge fireplace. From that day to this I've not touched a pendulum, yet there's no doubt that for some people they work amazingly well.

It's definitely worth trying out as many of the psychic tools available to us as possible before righting them off completely. We're all individuals, and each of ours psychic abilities will manifest in so many different ways. In any case, I don't think it matters too much what tools are being used as long as it's done with a passion and from the heart.

The next morning things were destined to get even more bizarre than just a rebellious pendulum. When I arrived in class everyone was clustered excitedly round the far end of the room, examining a black three-sided box, about the size of a photo-booth. Sharon informed the class the box was a 'cabinet'.

Cabinets are mostly used for physical mediumship. (I'm currently at time of writing this involved with sitting in a circle, working on developing physical mediumship – more about that later.) But at that particular time I didn't have any experience of this extremely rare and rather niche branch of mediumship.

Over the years I'd seen many old black and white photos of mediums sitting in cabinets in various states of trance, white materially-looking stuff called ectoplasm dripping from their nose and mouths, like some hugely mutated bogey. Yuck!

Personally, some of these old pictures look more than a little bit suspicious to me, but as I wasn't there I couldn't say for sure what was going on. I have read that some of these physical mediums were tested repeatedly under *extremely* strict conditions, and still produced incredible results.

All the same, these strange ancient photos always put me off looking too deeply in to physical mediumship – that was until I met a certain young man called Vince, who managed to convince me otherwise! But that wasn't destined to happen for another year or so yet.

As I stood staring at the cabinet, all the old photos I'd seen flashed through my mind. *Oh God, will we be expected to produce ectoplasm today? Surely not...*

I needn't have worried. The cabinet, the tutor explained, was going to be used for trance-work.

Apart from witnessing Pete going into trance five years back and the tutor on my first course here when a Chinese gentleman had made an appearance, I hadn't had much experience of trance mediumship. I'd certainly not tried it myself.

There was deadly silence as Sharon asked for a volunteer to be the first to sit in the cabinet.

'Come on, ladies, you never know, you might even enjoy it!' Sharon laughed. No one looked very convinced!

Her eyes came to rest on me. 'Up you get, Anne. Take a seat in the cabinet.'

'Yes, go on, Anne,' encouraged the others, no doubt relieved to be let off the hook.

'I won't disappear into Narnia if I go in there, will I?' I joked nervously.

Sharon chuckled. 'I shouldn't think so, although you never *quite* know what's going to happen in this place!'

Her remark hardly instilled me with confidence as I reluctantly pulled back the black curtain and stepped inside the cabinet. It felt really claustrophobic. Like many people, I'm not too great with enclosed spaces. Sharon pulled the curtains across, hiding me from view.

I felt a little panicky at first, which was silly really as I could leave any time I liked; it wasn't as if I was locked in. Funnily enough, after a minute or two it felt quite cosy sitting there with the curtains closed. A calm, sleepy feeling washed over me. Sharon had been right! It was really a very pleasant dreamy sensation – very relaxing, like getting a deep massage. It reminded me of the time I'd had healing off the Reiki-healer, Tony, a.k.a. Lizard-Guide-Man.

Sharon's mellow voice wafted through the curtain. 'Get yourself comfy, Anne, then ask for spirit to join you. There's no hurry. Take your time. In a moment I'm going to open the curtain so we can see how you're doing.'

Mentally, I asked my friends to draw as close to me as possible. I always do this when I'm doing any sort of psychic activity. Normally I'm on 'super-alert' when I'm reading; it's a very *active* energy. But this was completely different – very passive.

I became aware of a very gentle tickling sensation, which started at the top of my head, spread down to my cheeks, and finished at my chin. These were very real, tangible, physical sensations.

Being the ever-questioning sceptic, I wondered if I was experiencing these sensations because I was sitting so quietly. But since then I've sat still on a number of occasions, just to test myself, and not felt anything *close*. Sometimes, you just *have* to have faith in what you are feeling.

To my amazement I started to become extremely emotional. It was like I was sitting, wrapped up snugly in a blanket of pure love and compassion. I realise that this sounds as mushy as a *Mills and Boon* novel, but it's the only way to describe it.

At some point, I was vaguely aware of Sharon pulling open the curtain.

In hushed tones, the other students were commenting on what they could see or feel. It was like I was listening to what was being said, but I was very detached from the whole proceedings – a very weird sensation.

'If you feel any words forming just let them naturally flow from you,' Sharon instructed gently.

Words? What words? Did she expect me to speak in tongues?

This was where my old mate Panic made an unwelcome appearance.

All the wonderful floaty feelings I'd been enjoying so much suddenly felt like they'd been snatched away from me. My eyes popped open.

Sharon's voice was concerned 'Take your time, Anne. You came out of that far too quickly. Are you okay?'

I nodded, but felt really giddy and sick. Back at my seat, Sharon told me that for a first attempt at trance I'd had a really wonderful close 'blending' with spirit. Interestingly, three or four of the others had 'seen' the face of a Maori gentleman, but this was using their clairvoyant abilities. If it had been true physical mediumship *everyone* would've witnessed it.

Next up for the cabinet-experience was a lovely lady

called Barbara. Barbara suffered from a condition that caused her head to shake constantly.

Amazing as this sounds, when Barbara sat inside the cabinet within moments her head had stilled. All of us just sat watching with our jaws hanging open. How was this medically possible? I can only swear to you on my dad's grave that this miraculous event *did* happen.

When Barbara came out of the cabinet, she explained to us that this always happened to her when she was in an entranced state.

One by one everyone took their turn. It did cross my mind that if anyone could see a bunch of women spending a sunny, September day, staring at each other for hours whilst sitting about in a big black box, they might possible think we were just ever so slightly on the mad side! But, hey, what's sane?

It was actually quite fascinating observing the others as they 'sat'. I really enjoyed 'tuning in' and seeing who was around them.

'Get a good night's sleep tonight, ladies,' the grey-haired tutor advised us. 'We're going to do something *really* special tomorrow!'

On that enigmatic note we all headed off to the dining room for our well-earned dinner.

The food had been a bit of a talking point during the week, due to the fact that most of it had been classed as inedible by many of the students. Caroline's a vegetarian, and she wasn't too impressed with the meals being presented to her. I must admit, the bit I tried from her veggie-menu was about as tasty as a piece of cardboard.

That night in our room, Caroline and I decided, in true Enid Blyton style, to have a midnight feast!

I'd smuggled some fruit out of the dining room, and Caroline had popped to the local garage and picked up packets of biscuits and a number of various chocolate bars. (She's a self-confessed chocaholic!)

We sat up till after four in the morning chin-wagging, mostly about spiritual stuff, and steadily munching our way through the various goodies.

Finally, we gave our poor jaws a well-earned rest, and snuggled down for what was left of the night.

My eyes suddenly popped open. A very smartly dressed gentleman with a dark beard was hovering in front of me, a tiny smile on his distinguished face.

Seconds later, he was gone.

I groaned and turned over as the alarm went off. It couldn't be time to get up already?

'I think we ate too many biscuits last night,' Caroline mumbled, sitting up in bed. 'I saw a man in the room last night.'

I bolted upright.

'So did I! What did your man look like?'

'He was smartly dressed and had a beard.'

'Mine to!'

My God! This was *such* a revelation for me. I'd been seeing people for years, but no one had ever been able to back me up in my 'hallucinations'. My mum 'sees' people all the time, same as me, but I've never been in the same room as my mum on the same night to see if our 'visions' matched (although this has actually occurred since, but more on that later).

A more detailed conversation with Caroline left me convinced that we'd seen the same gentleman.

This was incredible! Someone had finally given me concrete conformation that I wasn't just imagining my regular nightly visitors.

Caroline was also gobsmacked. It was good evidence for both of us.

The day had started well, but was about to get even *better*...

14

Angelic Experiences

'I wonder what's in store for us today?' Barbara grinned as we trooped in for our morning lesson.

I shrugged, smiling back. 'We were promised something special, so who knows...?'

We soon found out.

'This morning we're going to try some *physical* mediumship, ladies!' said Sharon, her eyes glinting in the semi-darkened room. 'Has anyone here ever done any table-tilting before?'

I was really surprised when most of the others said that they *had* experienced table-tilting. Apart from myself, only another quite young lady – whose name I can't recall – hadn't tried it.

'Strictly speaking we're not allowed to do this,' Sharon told us, giving a conspiratorial wink. 'But rules are sometimes made to be broken!'

She fetched a small but solid looking table from the corner of the room. *It looks innocent enough*, I thought, as she plonked it in the centre of the library.

As instructed, we stood up and lightly placed our fingertips on the edge of the table.

Then, to my surprise, the tutors started to belt out a rendition of *Daisy, Daisy*! Everyone joined in. I muttered and spluttered my way through it, singing not being my strongest point.

As the singing increased in volume, I could feel the table starting to shake ever so slightly under my fingertips.

'That's it! Come forward, friends!' encouraged the grey-haired tutor.

We sung a couple more songs at the top of our voices. Suddenly, the table started to go mad. We could hardly keep up with the thing as it danced erratically round the room.

Me being 'Miss Sceptical' I watched everyone in turn, but couldn't work out how anyone could be moving it. It was quite a heavy table and we were only touching it extremely lightly.

The young girl was completely freaked out by what she was witnessing. She didn't like it one little bit and decided to leave the room.

'Does anyone else want to leave?' Sharon asked us in concern. 'How about you, Anne? You've not seen this before, have you?'

'I'm fine,' I quickly assured her. There was NO WAY I was going to miss out on all the fun. Wild spirits couldn't have dragged me away!

We quickly established a code for 'Yes' and 'No', and also a way of going through the alphabet. Then the party *really* got started. The table edged towards whomever it wanted to 'talk' to. Then it spelt out the name of the spirit trying to communicate. The person who was getting the message had to take their hands off the table so they couldn't influence it subconsciously. Each of us in turn received a message. As specific names and personal details were spelt out, a few of us, understandably, got quite emotional.

Before long the table was edging its way towards me! Gently it nudged my side like an affectionate puppy.

'Take your hands off, Anne,' Sharon instructed. 'Let's see who wants a little chat with you.'

I waited patiently as it went through its laborious alphabet routine, holding my breath, hoping it would stop at 'F' for Fred – my dad. But no, it stopped at 'N'. I racked my brains trying to think of someone that I knew beginning with 'N'. No one sprung to mind. Soon enough though, everything became clear when an 'A' and 'N' were also spelt out.

It was Nan. I couldn't feel her like I normally do when she's about, but then again I was new to this form of communication.

I must admit, I was a little disappointed that Nan's first name hadn't been spelt out, as the others had had, but I soon shrugged it off. It didn't really matter that much. After all, I'd had enough personal evidence given to me over the years to last a lifetime.

My eyes were glued to the table as I waited for the message from Nan to be revealed. I was so engrossed that if a ten-piece brass band, complete with conductor, had burst into the room to accompany our singing I wouldn't have noticed.

My message was finally spelt out.

S O P R O U D.

Sharon smiled. 'Ahh, that's lovely. She's proud of you.'

The table jiggled about in agreement, looking like it was auditioning for a part in *River-dance*.

The rest of the lesson was a blur for me. At lunch the whole dinner table listened agog as I relayed our morning 'table-dancing' session.

This course was definitely turning out to be a host of first time experiences for me, as I also got a taste of the well-known phenomena EVP – Electronic Voice Phenomena, the day after the table-tilting.

On my course was a dark-haired lady called Margaret. I had had quite a few in-depth chats with her over the week, and she'd struck me as being an extremely clued-up, educated individual. In some respects I think that she was still on the 'psychic-fence' when it came to spiritual things in general, but was open-minded enough to attend this course with a friend of hers. I'd noticed she had a habit of analysing everything rationally, which to my mind is a very healthy thing to do. I would much rather that than someone who believed every single word uttered by mediums, never questioning or challenging anything.

After lunch one day, she burst into the class, her face glowing. 'I've just listened to the tape of my reading with Sharon and there's a spirit voice on it,' she told us excitedly.

'It's as clear as anything. Listen to this!'

We all crowded round Margaret, eager to hear what'd been said. Sharon was there and was as astonished and curious as the rest of us.

Margaret pressed play and Sharon's distinct tone could immediately be heard describing a gentleman she was attempting to link with.

Then, talking over her, a man's deep voice said in a distinct Irish accent; '*I need to talk*!'

We played it several times and each time it was shockingly clear.

'Who *is* that, Sharon?' asked Margaret, puzzled. 'We were the only ones in there, and that man's *definitely* in the room.'

Sharon nodded. 'Does it sound like anyone you know in the spirit world?'

'It could be my granddad. He was Irish. But I don't remember his voice.'

What the gentleman 'needed to talk' about I doubt that we shall ever know. Margaret was going to play the tape to her older relatives in hope that they would be able to identify the owner of the mysterious voice.

The trouble with having such an *amazing* week is that it makes going back to real-life that much harder!

This course had opened my mind to other forms of mediumship to such an extent that as soon as I got home I booked another course, concentrating just on trance-mediumship, for the following February. My ambition was to try and let Spirit talk *through* me without my old mates Panic and Fear doing their usual trick and getting in the way.

I'd been back a week or so when I received devastating news.

I got a phone-call from Diane's husband, Mick. Diane had passed away. She was only in her mid-forties. She'd been in hospital for an infection of some kind, and had caught the superbug MRSA.

When Mick told me the details I was in such shock I just couldn't take it in. All I knew was that I'd been speaking to Diane on the phone just the previous month, and she'd been absolutely fine, laughing and joking as usual. Now she was gone.

Andy and I attended her funeral service up in Preston. It shocked me how upset I felt at her passing. Since she and my brother Rick had divorced I hadn't seen her very often as she'd gone to live back up north, but we'd stayed in close contact, especially during the 'aloe vera' period in our lives. I still think that if Diane hadn't contacted me about the aloe vera business, I probably wouldn't have become a reader. But, then again, you never know for sure, do you? Spirit always find a way if it's meant to be!

Still, in my mind, she'd been a major influence in my life. She was such an amazing and inspirational lady.

I asked my spirit friends if Diane was okay, and was assured that she was fine, but didn't get any additional information on her – much to my frustration.

I do very occasionally 'see' Bluebells; a flower I've always associated with Diane as she used to take me Bluebell picking in the woods near my home in Walton-on-Thames. It would be too easy for me to just assume that this is Diane, when it might not be. Spirit do seem to love their flowers, and often I see them floating about in my room after I've done a particularly intense reading. (God help anyone with hay-fever when they get to the spiritual-realms – the place is full of 'em!)

I know I must sometimes sound like a demanding five-year-old, asking this and that from Spirit, but usually if they *can* help me out they will. *Even* spirit haven't got *all* the answers – or if they have there are valid reasons they can't tell us everything we want to know.

Being nosy, I'm constantly asking That Lot questions

about the Spirit-World. I've always been dead curious when it comes to the next phase of life.

What did they do all day? Did they work over there? Did they get bored? What if they got tired of Eternity? And of course the big question – was there *really* a hell?

I've read many books on the subject of the afterlife, but I wanted to hear it from the horse's mouth, so to speak. When spirit people come to talk to their loved ones, I always enjoy a natter with them about their new environment.

In my first year of reading I'll never forget a gentleman I linked with called Ken. I was reading for his wife, and as usual was trying my hardest to get through as much evidence as possible. She suddenly stopped me in mid-sentence and said she only wanted to know one thing; was Ken happy in his new life?

'I am now I'm away from her constant nagging!' He quipped cheekily in my ear. When I reluctantly repeated this she thankfully gave a hearty laugh.

'Yes, I'm great,' Ken assured me. Then he showed me a vivid picture of a very cosy looking cottage he was now living in. I don't know why it surprised me, but it did. I kind of had these images of spirit people all living together in some sort of great temple made of pure golden light. But here was an ordinary guy living in an ordinary cottage, proudly informing me that he built it himself with 'particles of light' and using the power of 'directive thought'!

Apparently, in *their* world, *Thoughts* are extremely important. In *our* world everything starts with a thought, but it takes time and action to manifest our thoughts into reality. Over there they use *thought-energy* to create what they want. It's not instantaneous, but it's much quicker than our world.

For a long time I've believed that there is some sort of link between quantum physics and the spiritual dimensions. Only trouble is I'm not brainy enough to figure out what the exact link is and how it all works. Spirit have told me that the realities of consciousness living outside the physical body, and the fact that other dimensions exist, would be found in this branch of science.

Every time I try and read up on quantum mechanics I can feel my brain starting to slowly sizzle away as if it's a piece of meat being cooked at a barbecue. Consequently, I dare not read past chapter two on any material covering this immense subject!

The many chats I've had over the years with various spirit people explain that when they first pass over the thing that strikes them most is the overall feeling of arriving home, and being surrounded in pure love. Yes, this might sound incredibly corny, but sometimes corny is good!

Every spirit person seems to have a unique experience once reaching the next life. One lady told me she was handed by her father a kind of 'Welcome to Spirit' pamphlet, complete with '3D pictures', when she'd first arrived. (I wasn't too sure if she was serious or joking!)

My guides have told me that the place Ken's in is the closest to Earth, but there are countless spheres, realms, dimensions, whatever you want to call them, over there.

A few years ago, I started getting quite a lot of information pouring into my mind regarding the higher realms. I linked with a gentleman called Edgar who had died over a hundred years ago. Whilst on earth he wasn't the nicest person to know, and it's fair to say he had a little bit of a shock when he passed over. He seemed eager to share with me his experiences regarding the struggles he'd had to overcome in the spiritual world. I found linking with him quite an emotional experience and, at the time, couldn't handle it. Now I'm stronger I might ask him to come back and share with me his earthy memories and what he's leant since passing over – but that's hopefully another book!

The soul is always striving to improve itself. Most spirit people I've spoken to seem to be chirpy, alive and full of laughter, so I can only assume they're enjoying their new life.

Occasionally I've linked with someone who, when alive, caused great pain to others, like Edgar, and are now full of regret. No, they don't tell me that they're being prodded by horned-demons with pitchforks. They are in a place where they can contemplate their mistakes, and hopefully make amends for them by making useful contributions to those that they've hurt, and Mankind in general. Every help and form of guidance is offered to them during this difficult period in their spiritual development.

Quite often, I'm asked the same question every medium on the face of the planet is probably asked; are our loved ones our guardian angles?

I suppose it depends how you define a 'guardian angel'.

Enough books have been written about angels to keep anyone interested in them happy to the next millennium. I must admit, there seems to be so much conflicting information out there, I'm completely bamboozled by the whole 'angel thing'. I deal with loved-ones and guides, any higher than that and I get a little nervous.

Everyone must interpret angels in their own way, but in writing this I asked Honrad to tell me – in his opinion – a little bit about them.

This is what I received:

Angels is a term used to call highly evolved souls who have volunteered to help those on your planet. They are the embodiment of compassion, understanding and love. Whatever humans have suffered they too have suffered. Please don't think of angles as beautiful, winged beings who've lived blessed, unblemished lives. That would be a mistake. Their souls have experienced every negative emotion you could ever come across in your world – but also every positive one.

Some on your world believe that angels are too spiritually evolved to enter the dark, terrible places of your planet, but this is not the case. This is where you are most likely to find angels – where there is darkness, ignorance and despair. They are tireless in their purpose; which is to bring hope, healing and enlightenment to humankind.

I realise this information on angels is very basic, but I want this book to reflect my own *personal* experiences, and I'm afraid when it comes to the angelic-kingdom it's pretty limited. Although I *do* have two experiences that I would love to share with you.

The first happened about three or so years ago. I was absolutely exhausted, mentally and physically, after doing a heavy few weeks of very long and intense readings.

Andy decided that he would give me a little healing, but gave up after I succumbed to a mad giggling fit (I'm prone to these at the most inappropriate moments) every time he attempted to administer the healing.

After his third attempt, he impatiently told me he'd send me an angel to help out instead. Maybe then I would take it a little more seriously!

That evening, I told my friend Vince about this dismal healing session, and he too promised to send an angel to help me regain my strength and energy.

One could argue that I had 'angels on the brain' as I closed my eyes and drifted off that night, and in fairness yes, this could be the case. But I don't believe that.

Although I couldn't see anyone, I was acutely aware of someone by my side. We were gliding together over endless miles of countryside. As I looked down at the scenery whizzing by, the amazing vibrant colours and unusual contours of the landscape totally stunned me. It reminded me of one of those colourful fantasy-world pictures gifted people paint.

I kept trying to glance at the 'Being' travelling alongside me, but just couldn't seem to see him or her. Whilst we were flying along, sensations of the most incredible contentment rippled constantly thorough me. This is so hard to explain.

It was just such a wonderful feeling and I hate not being able to give the experience true justice. Yet again, words seem so totally inadequate, but I'm doing my very best here.

My travelling companion didn't utter one word to me as we continued on our ethic journey. No words were needed. I knew instinctively that the immense peace and warmth I was enjoying so much were emanating from the 'Being'.

He or she just radiated the highest, purest feeling of well-being you could possibly imagine. I would've quite happily stayed with them for all of time! Of that there is *no doubt* in my mind.

The weeks following my 'dream' I found I felt so much happier and stronger; better than I'd been for ages.

I'm still unsure whether to use the word 'angel' to describe my silent travelling friend. I certainly didn't spot any wings, even if we were flying!

The other experience I had was when I went to read for a lady who was on holiday near my home with her severely disabled husband who I shall call John.

John sat by me in his wheelchair as I read for his wife. I'm pretty sure he was oblivious to what was going on. The reading went very well, and the evidence and messages were flowing nicely from her mum and dad and other relatives. Quite suddenly, I was clearly aware of this huge 'Being' standing directly behind John's wheelchair.

At first, I was unsure whether the Being had been there all along or had just appeared at that moment. When asked, I was told the Being had been there from the moment John had had the accident which had condemned him to the life he now led.

If John, trapped in his useless body, was experiencing the joy I'd experienced at the sheer presence of these Beings, then in a way I envied him. But of course I can't tell you for sure what he was experiencing. I can only pray that he *was* enjoying the peace and contentment I felt for a few short precious minutes that night.

The only other story I can think of relating to angels, is about a spirit gentleman who came back to see me after I linked with him for his lovely daughter, Katie.

It's quite rare that after a reading the spirit person will come back into my consciousness, but when Katie had gone, I was surprised to recognise the man's voice as I sat relaxing with a well-deserved KitKat. He thanked me for passing his messages to her, then he said; '*Over here we call mediums Earth Angels! You are our little Earth Angel, Anne.*'

I must admit, I did shed a tear or two. It just seemed such a lovely thing to call us. I wondered if anyone else had heard of this term for mediums, but no one I asked seemed to be familiar with it.

I do get a little cross when people insist that angels find them parking spaces or something just as trivial. An angel expert I do not claim to be, but surely if someone is going to be call upon these amazing beings, shouldn't it be over something truly worthy of their attention? Just my opinion.

Another question I'm frequently asked is; 'Do your own loved ones visit you, Anne?'

Of course, the answer is yes, they do.

I constantly sense Nan and Dad around me, and I've been privileged enough on occasion, to have actually *seen* them.

Since my late teens I've seen spirit people in an objective way. They appear outside myself and are as real and solid as any live person. I'm not talking about vague shadowy figures, or even orbs. I'm talking about crystal-clear, full-blown people. My mum also sees spirit people like I do. When this first happened, I clearly remember almost being scared to death. I was sitting up in bed, yelling at this man standing in my room. I thought it was a burglar.

I'm NOT asleep when this happens – I'm *completely* conscious. I did used to wonder if I might have some sort of brain disorder, but I think I've been given enough evidence over the years to rule this out.

Once I woke up to see a man, slightly bent over, staring intently into my glass of water, which was on my bedside table. He disappeared – thank God – when I switched on my lamp. When I picked my glass up to see what had fascinated him so much, I noticed a moth flapping about in the glass.

I was truly amazed. He'd been observing something I didn't even know was there! This proved (to my mind) that he wasn't just a 'figment of my imagination'!

Apart from my mum, I've never spoken to anyone who sees regularly in this way. I think most mediums 'see' spirit people in their mind's eye, and this is the way I see them when I'm giving a reading.

I don't know how common this 'objective seeing' phenomena is amongst the general public. Maybe it's very common but no one wants to admit it in case they're labelled crazy or deluded. I've had around ten clients confide in me that they've physically seen spirit, but it's always been people they've known, and usually at times they've really needed it.

As a child, I clearly remember my nan telling me of the time Spirit had visited her.

'One night my deceased mother appeared to me,' Nan said in her soft voice. 'I was going through an extremely difficult time. Granddad had lost his job, and we were about to be made homeless. I was pregnant with Uncle Norman, and your mum was very ill. My mother, Amelia, who'd died quite young, appeared to me, took my hand, and promised that in the morning everything would be fine.'

The next day Nan told me that the prophecy turned out to be true, as my granddad found work, and Mum had got better. Nan was eternally grateful to her mother for the reassurance she'd given her when she'd truly needed it.

A lady I read for a few years ago told me she'd woken one night to see, to her astonishment, her long deceased grandmother standing at the side of her bed. The next morning she received the news that her son had been killed in a road accident. She confided in me that the vision of her beloved granny had given her hope and unbelievable comfort. She knew her son was okay and being looked after by Granny.

I've seen literally thousands of people who I don't recognise, and it's always been very sporadic. The exceptions are the time I saw my guide, Honrad, which was in answer to a direct request from me.

I've also seen Dad and Nan, and just recently I've seen Uncle Ronnie, my mum's brother, who brought us the carpet I had a dream about as a child.

The first – and only time – I've *physically* seen Dad was a year or so after I started as a professional reader. It was about ten months after the medium, Mary, had drawn his picture.

I opened my eyes one night, and there he was – his familiar face hovering in front of me. In shock, I propped myself up and stared at him. As I watched, and this is quite difficult to explain, something like a bluish coloured tube protruded from the middle of his forehead. He was smiling gently at me and I didn't feel scared, just surprised and confused.

The word 'third-eye' popped into my mind. The weeks that followed I noticed that when I was reading I was 'seeing' pictures in my mind a lot sharper and clearer than before. I believe that somehow Dad had helped me with my 'inner-vision' so I could obtain more evidence and details when giving a reading.

Nan made her first appearance to me around six years ago. I'd been chatting to her loads one day, asking her questions about her life in the spirit world. At the end of the conversation I asked Nan to show herself to me if what I'd heard back really *was* her and not my sub-conscious feeding me the answers I wanted to hear. She didn't let me down. That night, there she was, but like Dad, I only saw her head and shoulders.

The other time I saw Nan was last year. I opened my eyes and again, there she was, just her face, beaming down at me. The next day I realised it'd been her birthday. To my shame I'd forgotten. (Maybe she'd come to collect her pressie! Sorry Nan!)

I've noticed that there seems to be two different ways I see spirit people. Some of them are standing, or gliding, in the room, and are fully formed. And with the other ones I only see the upper part of their bodies and faces. These ones appear to be peering in through a window. It's like the fabric of space opens up a little and there they are.

Once I saw an Indian boy of about seven, who was sitting crossed-legged in one of these 'windows' staring down at me out of huge liquid brown eyes. I noticed he was wearing a half-gold, half-purple turban. I don't know who he was, and haven't seen him since. I did wonder if he could be a guide of mine, but don't think he is. The thing I clearly remember from this vision is the activity taking place in the background. I could see people milling around, no doubt going about their spiritual business. But the thing that struck me was the beauty of the colours and textures of that world. Looking back, I believe I was getting a glimpse into the spiritual realms – same as in my 'angel-dream'.

Once, I asked Honrad about some of the people I see that I don't recognise, and was given an extremely surprising answer. It was *so* unexpected I'm still unsure whether to completely believe it.

I was informed that I was, in effect, being 'used' by spirit people whilst they had a 'practise-run' appearing in our world. They came to me before they toddled off to shock their relatives – as in the case of the lady who'd been shocked, but comforted, by her grandmother's appearance.

I can only assume that this also applies to my mum. Apparently, we volunteered for this important service!

Mum once confided in me that when we were living in Walton, just before we moved to Guildford, she used to see many faces with concerned expressions staring down at Dad. He must've had cancer at the time, but of course we didn't know that fact until much later. I can only assume they were there sending him some sort of healing.

Not long ago I saw a cute little girl of around three or four, standing right by my bed. She almost shocked me to death she was so close and so clear.

Her hair was a vivid shade of strawberry blonde. I've never seen that *exact* shade on anyone else. She had the cutest little face and was grinning away cheekily. She kept ducking down and popped up again, like she was playing 'peek-a-boo' with me.

I said; '*Hello, there*,' to her, but she didn't reply. Then she faded away. I can't portray here the sheer joy that just seemed to radiate from this little girl's very Being. I don't see many spirit children, so it was a real surprise to have this wonderful experience.

The next day I rang Mum to tell her about my visitor, but before I had the chance, she started to tell *me* about the little girl *she* had seen in the night.

I listened, feeling totally shocked. The description of Mum's little girl tallied exactly with mine. She'd visited *both of us*, based in different locations, on the same night!

Believe me, I question *everything* I experience, but this was such great, personal evidence for me that I'm not completely round the twist. Of course it had happened once before, with my mate, Caroline, but this was even stronger and better than that time.

I'm so used to seeing strangers appear I often wonder what I would do if real live intruders were in my room. I would probably just assume they were spirit people and give my usual greeting of; '*Hello, welcome friends*,' which might confuse them just a bit!

Apart from the crowds of people that visit me, I also see objects.

It would take far too long to write about all the various objects I've seen over the past twenty years. I could fill a book on that alone, but it would be pretty boring. The very first thing I saw was the green and white striped shirt at my partner Robert's house – that later turned up on Andy on our first date. Many times I've seen something and the next day the object has appeared in real life.

This has happened to me a countless number of times. A prime example of this was the time I woke up only to see millions of tiny particles of blue and purple light, shimmering like glitter. As I watched, hypnotised, the pinpoints of light arranged themselves into an incredibly beautiful swirly pattern. Each part of this complex pattern was slowly rotating, and the overall effect was just *stunning*.

The next day I was in the post office when Andy called me over to look at a postcard that had caught his eye. I was astonished to be faced with the *exact same image I'd witnessed the previous night*. No sceptic in the world could tell me that this was pure coincidence.

Andy told me the picture was of a fractal. He then when on to tell me (being the clever-clogs that he is) that this is an infinitely repeating mathematical pattern!

I'd never even heard of a flipping fractal, but apparently they're everywhere in nature.

The only conclusion I can come to regarding these little peeks into the future, is that spirit wanted me to have as much evidence as possible into the reality of their existence. Altogether, it built up a very powerful library of 'paranormal memories' that gave me the faith to become a medium.

I don't think I could've had that strong believe without the experiences that I've encountered along the way to back it up.

Most of my visions are never repeated, but there have been a couple of things that have 'haunted' me throughout the years.

The first thing is a video camera. I first saw it just after my dad passed away, and have seen it around twenty times a year. I'm unsure whether it's connected with Dad as one of the last things he said was he'd keep an eye on me. (But I don't think he'd do it through a camera!)

A very respected medium once told me that it was a security camera, and represented protection for me, but this didn't ring true. The weird thing is, the camera looks different each time I see it. Sometimes it looks antique, and sometimes futuristic. It always appears randomly, sometimes days in a row, then not for months at a time, and it's always pointing directly at me, which is a little bit disconcerting!

To this day I have no real clue whatsoever to the origins or meaning of this regular intrusion in my life. I did a little automatic writing a year or so ago, and had some very wacky and interesting ideas presented to me regarding my development with physical mediumship, but I took it with a pinch of salt.

(Anyone out there with any thoughts on my on-going camera mystery? Answers on a postcard, please!)

The other thing I see fairly regularly (although not as regular as Old Faithful – the camera) is this very strange shiny black machinery. Sometimes it almost fills the whole room; sometimes it's only as big as a shoe-box, but it's always inky-black, shiny and high-tech looking. My mum has also seen this weird looking machinery. I was worried about including this in my book, because it sounds so 'out-there' but it's what I have witnessed and I want to share as many of my experiences as possible with people. Yet again, I have no real answers to give you on the meaning of the machinery.

I would be very curious to find out if anyone else has seen anything like this. Please let me know if you have.

In the winter of '05 I attended my first proper trance mediumship course back at the college in Essex.

It was extremely interesting to learn about this branch of mediumship, and I did actually speak a few words on this very unusual week. Sorry to disappoint, but it was nothing earth-shattering. It was on the lines of '*Good afternoon to you all. It's a real pleasure to be here'*.

Without wanting to sound negative, I found watching some of the other students a little disturbing. There seemed to be, in my eyes, a lot of pulling funny-faces and animalistic grunting going on. It was fascinating and frankly pretty scary, hearing the 'spirit communicators' speaking through some of the other students.

One of them, a young guy, even managed to 'channel' through a little old lady called Doris, who was in a nearby old folk's home, and was just about to – in her words – 'snuff it'! (I'm not joking.)

I must admit, I was just a tinsy bit sceptical that some of these people were truly being inspired by higher minds!

With normal mediumship the facts tend to speak for themselves.

I once read that someone (I think it was a well-known scientist) said; '*Remarkable claims require remarkable proof*', and this had always stuck in my mind. Mediums and psychics *do* make pretty huge claims – that they can communicate with the dead. So there *has* to be remarkable, or at least some sort of evidence, to back that claim up.

If you say 'I've got your Great Auntie Gertrude communicating here, who passed over on Christmas day after choking on a Brussels sprout', or whatever, no one can argue with it. But with *trance* there are hardly any *facts* mentioned. It's more what would be termed as philosophical in its content.

So *exactly* what source the information is coming from is difficult to determine. I must admit, in my meaner more sceptical moments, I wondered if certain people were drawn to trance because they just couldn't deliver the cold hard facts that normal mediumship expects and demands.

The only judge can be the common sense of individual observing the trance mediumship.

Towards the end of the week my hope was restored (thank God) when two of the tutors gave us a demonstration of trance, which, similar to the very first course I'd attended here, blew me away!

Admittedly, not so much with the evidence, but with the very real physical tingly-electricity sensations as they went in and out of the trance state, and with the quality of the content of the messages from their spirit-team.

It was a pure joy to witness.

In fact, I was so impressed with the tutors and the course in general that I booked for the following year. I really wanted to see if I could get to say more than just the pleasantries of '*Good afternoon, friends*'.

I very nearly cancelled this course as money was, as per usual, a little tight. Thank God I didn't – because I met Vince...

15

Meeting Vince. Losing Gina

It's funny how some people cross our paths for a short time and others you instinctively know will *always* be around. That's how I feel about my best friend in the whole world, Vince.

Vince is most definitely not your average guy

For a start you can't really miss him! He's six foot two and rather a large build, although not in an overweight way. He's just naturally big. He has very distinct black tribal tattoos on his forearms, and a closely-shaven head. First time I saw him he was wearing ripped jeans and a casual flimsy T-shirt, even though it was in freezing February.

People tend to judge him on how he looks, and that week wasn't any different. I noticed the suspicious looking glances he was getting from the other students, and the fact they were obviously avoiding him

On the first evening in the bar, he cut a very forlorn and lonely picture, sitting all by himself, nursing a can of Guinness and fiddling with his phone.

I was sat at a table with a couple of people I knew from other courses. As Vince got up to leave, the lady sitting with me called him over to join us for a drink, which, grinning shyly, he did.

Naturally most of the conversation was based around spiritual matters, and I was totally blown-away on the depth of knowledge this young man (well, younger than me, anyway) possessed.

It transpired that Vince was on the advanced mediumship course, whereas I was on the trance one. So we would be attending different classes.

Vince told us he had run a few psychic and mediumship development workshops, and had also given some private one-to-one readings.

'I can see you're a working medium by your really powerful eyes,' he blurted out, as I carried back a round of drinks from the bar.

This surprised me because no one at the college had ever picked up on the fact that I worked as a full time medium. Most people attending the college have 'normal' jobs. On these courses I never like to volunteer the fact I'm a professional medium. Firstly, because I feel like it puts me under pressure in class to perform. And secondly, everyone always wants mini-readings off me when they find out, and when I'm away on these courses they work you so hard it's nice to just chill in the evenings with a nice glass of red wine. Not spend all night giving readings!

I was impressed (and secretly pleased) with Vince sussing me out at lightning speed. (Unless of course my eyes just *seemed* to be powerful because they were glazed over as I was a bit tipsy!)

As the week progressed, Vince and I had many chats together during the breaks and in the evenings, and I was so amazed and delighted to meet someone who seemed to share so many similar views to myself regarding mediumship and so many other related subjects.

I've met many people within the spiritual community and, believe me, some of them have some extremely 'way-out and wacky' beliefs, which of course is completely fine. I'm sure *my* beliefs are pretty 'out-there' to a lot of people, and I understand that. But to meet someone on the *exact* same wavelength as myself was so unbelievably refreshing.

We discussed so many wonderful subjects, and he really opened up my mind in so many unexpected and amazing ways. I'm usually quite weak at verbally putting across my thoughts and opinions to people, but with Vince I found I didn't have that problem. He actually *listened* to what I had to say, and I could see he truly respected and agreed with most of it.

He was here to advance his mental mediumship, and had already blown away most of the other students with his platform demonstration. Whereas at first they'd been wary of him, now he was being looked upon with almost a reverence from the other students. Which proves the old saying – never judge a book by its cover!

I had a trance-healing session booked near the end of the week, and asked Vince if he would be kind enough to sit in on the session with me. We had to be chaperoned for legal reasons.

I was having the healing done because for the last six months I'd suffered the really horrible sensation of a huge lump in my throat. It sometimes felt like a hand was tightly gripping my throat. I'd also lost a stone in weight (which was the only plus point) but I would rather be back at my usual weight and not have to suffer this awful lumpy feeling. I'd had a camera put down my throat, but nothing could be found. I was just at my wits' end.

I'd never experienced trance-healing and wondered if it would be similar to the Reiki I'd had in the past.

The female tutor giving the healing popped me up onto the therapist's couch, then went into trance. Within minutes the spirit doctor who was working alongside her 'blended' with his medium and started to have a little chat with me regarding my condition.

Not a massive amount was said, but it did make sense to me. More importantly, the healing I received felt very powerful. I could picture the doctor quite clearly in my head: a grey-haired, smartly dressed and very distinguished-looking gentleman in his sixties.

Afterwards (before I said anything) Vince described the same man to me. I can imagine that the sceptics would say what we both described would be a typical image of a respectable doctor. Maybe that's true, but I *physically* saw this gentleman on three separate occasions over the following year, and he looked just like we'd described him. He appeared to me when I'd been suffering with my asthma problems again. I had appealed directly to him to help me. He told me that as I was now one of patients he would visit from time to time to administer extra healing.

Thank you, Doc, I really appreciated it.

As for my lumpy throat, Vince also gave me a few healing sessions, and although it took another few months, it did slowly start to get better from that point on. Yes, it's true that it might've recovered anyway, given enough time, but I truly believe the healing gave my body the kick-start it needed to heal itself.

In the summer of '06 my mum, big brother, Steve, and his partner, Gina, came to stay with us. Steve and Gina had been together for about twelve years, and quite often popped down to stay with us.

I got on extremely well with Gina. It would be almost impossible *not* to get on with her, as she was such a gentle, good-natured lady.

We spent a wonderful Saturday afternoon taking a stroll by the sea, having our photo taken with Bugs-Bunny (don't ask – Mum insisted) and playing monopoly – a family favourite. In the evening we ordered our usual Indian take-away.

We were all stuffed full to bursting, apart from Steve, who was still nibbling the remnants of the coconut Nan, dipped in mango chutney. (He's fondly known as 'The Stomach' in our family due to his amazing ability to eat without ever seeming to get full-up!) Gina started to discuss my work as a medium. The subject always surfaced at some point when they came to stay. Steve's always been a sceptic on all spiritual matters, and he and I have had many friendly debates over the years (in a nutshell he thinks I'm crazy). My other brother, Rick, is the total opposite. He *completely* believes in it all, and is an amazing psychic and healer.

Gina loved to ask me questions about my life as a medium, and my opinions on what comes next after this world. Every time I saw her she asked me for a reading. It was always said jokingly, because I knew she didn't want to put me under any pressure.

'You always read for Steve, but not me!' she would grumble. I knew she was half-teasing, but I could tell she really *did* want a reading from me.

It was true that I *had* picked up tiny bits and pieces for Steve. I'd actually linked with Dad once for him. Out of all of us, Steve was closest to Dad as they worked together for many years. One day, before I'd become a professional reader, Steve had been challenging me regarding my so-called psychic abilities.

'Give me something specific and not just some vague rubbish that can apply to anyone. *Then* I might believe there's something in it!'

I immediately heard a voice in my head saying. '*Mention Max the dog.*' I'm certain that the voice I heard was Dad's.

When I repeated this to Steve, his face paled. 'I started a new job today and Max *is* the name of dog they've got.'

'Dad was there with you,' I said quietly.

This was significant because Dad hadn't been gone long, and Steve was now running the business on his own. He missed Dad so much as they'd always worked together.

He didn't comment much, but just kept giving me puzzled glances. I *have to stress* that there is *no way* I could've known this information, and I am reporting it exactly how it was said.

From that day to this I only have to say to Steve '*Remember Max the dog*!' and he immediately shuts up. It's marvellous – like having my very own remote control where I can press the mute button to his mouth!

Gina wanted a life reading off me, as she wanted to change her work, and there were also 'other things' she said she needed some guidance on.

I told her that I couldn't read for her, as I knew her *far* too well. The least I know about someone the better it obviously is – or so I believed at that time. Ironically, time would prove me wrong on *that* particular opinion.

Five years on and it still haunts me that maybe I *should've* given Gina the reading and guidance she so desperately needed that August day.

But I didn't.

Five short months later Gina passed to Spirit, taken from us, like so many others, by cancer. She was just 51.

We had no clue that she was so ill until just a few weeks before her passing.

Why hadn't I picked up what was going on whilst we sat there laughing and joking, playing board games? It might've just given her time to have treatment.

I WAS SUPPOSED TO BE PSYCHIC, WASN'T I?

And if I'd given her the reading she'd wanted, *maybe* I would've picked something up. But that's something I will never know...

My poor brother was totally inconsolable. I know this is *completely untrue*, but I felt my family and friends were silently wondering why I hadn't picked up anything about Gina's illness.

Vince was such an amazing and supportive friend to me during this awful time.

As a fellow medium, I felt he was the only one who I could share my anger and confusion with on the fact that I hadn't sensed something so important. It seemed a sick joke to me that I could pick up so much weird and wonderful stuff for other people, but not for our own beautiful Gina.

Vince told me he suspected I wasn't *supposed* to have access to information of that kind. There could be a thousand and one reasons why I hadn't been given anything on Gina's illness. Deep down I kind of already knew and understood what he was saying, but I so much appreciated his wise and deeply comforting words.

I also asked my guides why I hadn't been given any information that might have saved her, but I can't remember receiving any reply. I'm sure I would remember if I had.

One incident, which I really wanted to mention, happened the night Gina passed over. I opened my eyes and hovering above me was a radiant ball of golden light. I didn't note down the time, but it was around three in the morning.

The exact moment of Gina's passing will never be known, but I knew as soon as I saw the ball of light that Gina had passed over safely and was okay. Amazingly, Gina's daughter-in-law, a lady with no connections to spiritual matters, told me at the funeral that she'd also seen a globe of gold that night.

A few weeks after the funeral, Steve and Mum came to stay with us.

It was so heart-breaking to watch my lovely brother going through so much pain and grief. All the people I had tried my hardest to help over the years, but now there didn't seem to be anything I could do to help my own brother. Or was there...?

16

Gina's Return

It happened quite naturally.

Steve, Mum, Andy and I were sitting in the lounge sipping our coffee, when suddenly I was aware that Gina was standing next to me. I don't think I've ever felt a spirit person's presence so strongly. I couldn't see her objectively, but without a doubt she was there.

I'd had no plan in my mind to link with Gina that weekend; she'd only been gone a few weeks. But she'd decided to join us anyway.

At first I thought Gina was just going to give me a few general messages of comfort for Steve. After all, what evidence would I be able to get from her? I already *knew* all the usual stuff, such as way of passing over, name, age, job, hobbies, etc.

But Gina obviously knew that Steve would NOT be fobbed off with a few vague 'she's happy and watching over you' type comments, although these *are* valid comments when *backed up with evidence.*

The first thing she told me was to tell Steve she had 'Katie' with her. This really threw me because I had never heard of a Katie connected to Gina in any way. Steve looked a bit stunned. He told me Katie was Gina's sister's dog. Katie had passed over the same day as Gina.

She then said she'd seen someone called Barry fixing a door at their home recently. Steve told me Barry was Gina's brother-in-law, and he had been fixing the back door the previous day. Gina then jokingly told Steve to stop leaving the fridge door open, which he admitted he'd been doing a lot recently, and had even apologies to her out loud a day or two before, as he knew she used to grumble about it.

By this time Steve was giving Mum quite a few

suspicious glances, no doubt thinking that she was the source of my information, but Mum swore she didn't even know any of this stuff herself.

Altogether, there was over twenty separate pieces of extremely specific evidence. The very last thing Gina asked me to say before her voice faded was to thank Steve for the candles he'd been lighting for her every night since her passing. This puzzled me because I just couldn't visualise *Steve* lighting candles. Believe me – candles are definitely not his thing. Tentatively, I mentioned them, as Gina was so insistent.

Steve's reaction was immediate. Face bright red, he turned to Mum and blatantly accused her of feeding me the evidence from Gina.

It took some convincing that this was completely untrue. Of course I wouldn't deceive my own beloved brother in this way – or anyone else for that matter.

We wrote all the evidence down and, reading back through the list, the only thing he couldn't understand was a 'Maureen' who Gina insisted was going to help him on his road to recovery. (I secretly thought it could possibly be a new partner.)

After the reading, Andy took Steve through a guided meditation. On this meditation, Steve 'met' Gina and sat with her for a while in a peaceful garden.

As a rule my family don't really do 'emotional' that well; we're all quite shy, private people. But boy did Steve do 'emotional' during that meditation.

When he'd returned and the tears had subsided, he told us Gina had assured him she was well, and would be 'around', but she'd also encouraged him to 'be happy' in his new life without her.

The change in him after the reading and meditation was truly incredible. His whole demeanour was of a man who'd received an incredible amount of healing, and had now found new strength to start afresh.

Interestingly, the Maureen lady mentioned made an appearance in Steve's life a few weeks after the reading. She turned out to be a bereavement counsellor assigned to him, and she *did* help him quite a bit.

In the autumn of '06 (this was a few months before Gina passed away) I was back at my favourite place in good old Essex, on a course which was a mixture of mental mediumship, psychic stuff and a bit of trance thrown in for good measure.

A lot of the friends I'd collected over the years, including Vince, were on the course, and I could tell they'd be plenty of late nights in the bar with this particular rowdy crowd. (Excellent!)

The first morning down at breakfast we took our places – the same seats as the previous evening. Once seated we had to keep the same places all week. As we sat down I noticed a small package lying inconspicuously by Vince's plate.

'What's that?' a guy called Colin asked, tucking into his full English breakfast. 'Is it your birthday or something, mate?'

Vince shrugged and picked it up. We all watched as he unwrapped his present. It was a beautiful piece of amethyst crystal.

'Wow! Who gave you that?' Colin asked. 'It's gorgeous. Bet that cost a bit.'

Vince looked confused. 'Haven't a clue,' he shrugged. 'I don't know anyone here, apart from Anne. Amethyst's my favourite crystal.'

Everyone looked expectantly at me. I shook my head. 'Sorry, but not guilt.'

No one looked very convinced.

Nothing else was said, but when we all trooped into the dining room the next morning, yet again there was package waiting for Vince at his place.

'Someone must really like you, Vince!' Colin grinned. He gave me a cheeky wink. 'Wonder who it is?'

'Don't look at me!' I complained. 'It definitely isn't me. Honest.'

Bacon and eggs were left to congeal as all eyes focused on Vince and his mysterious package.

I'll never forget the incredulous look on Vince's face when the contents were revealed. It was a statuette of a gorgeous Buddha.

'I had one just like this but I gave it away to someone a few months back,' he told us in amazement. 'I was really fond of it.'

Again, I could feel all eyes on me. After all, as Vince had pointed out, no one here *knew* him, apart from yours truly. How would anyone realise how important crystals were to him? And how would they know he'd recently given away his Buddha? (In fact he'd given it to me – and I still have it – an *identical* Buddha!)

For the third consecutive morning, a new present appeared by his place. This time it was a large, pretty seashell.

Vince's eyes filled with tears. I knew from our chats how important the sea was to him. But once again, how would anyone here have known that fact?

We were all quite disappointed when come the next day there wasn't any goodies waiting on the table for Vince. Everyone seemed to have come to the *wrong* conclusion that I was the bearer of the secret gifts. Vince had told me he knew me well enough to know it *wasn't* me.

The three gifts were absolutely *perfect* for Vince, but who had *really* given them to him?

At a later date, Vince explained to me the *true* importance of his gifts. I won't go into detail, but in a nutshell they represented protection, enlightenment and communication to him.

The weeks preceding the course, Vince and I had been discussing physical mediumship quite a bit. We'd also spoken a lot about apports.

Apports are basically objects which spirit people take from one place and materialise in another. They don't steal anything, but take things that won't be missed by anyone. Of course we can never be absolutely sure, but we believe the three very meaningful gifts he received that week were apports.

Apport – sorry, I meant apart – from Vince's presents, it was a very relaxing and not too heavy week, where nothing spectacular happened. That was until the last but one day arrived...

All week the tutors had been working us up into a state of great excitement, promising us a real treat. Apparently, someone *very special* was due to arrive at the college to demonstrate his unique psychic abilities to us lesser mortals!

The air was electrifying as we took our seats in the crowded room. I could feel a flurry of exhilaration ripple through my tummy. What were we about to witness?

A small, dark-haired gentleman was introduced to us, and we were informed he had travelled all the way from South America to be here. A smartly-dressed lady, who was travelling with him, explained that the gentleman would be going into an entranced state and would be channelling through various artists – deceased, obviously! They would work 'through him' to create some masterpieces... hopefully! Not only that, but he would be timed to see how long each painting took him to complete.

So, paintbrushes waggling away at roughly the speed of light, off he went. Less than five minutes later, I think it was four minutes and twenty seconds, something like that, the first painting was ready for public inspection.

Murmurs and gasps of admiration circulated around the audience.

Accompanied by many 'ooohs' and 'ahhs', the smartly-dressed lady proudly carried the painting up and down the hall, holding it as lovingly as if it was her first born!

It was a wonderful scenic painting, full of vibrant colour. As you already know, I'm no expert in the Wonderful World of Art, but how on earth could someone paint such a gorgeous picture in less than five minutes?

I can't remember how long the second picture took to complete, but I know it was just a few minutes. I *do* remember thinking that it was even more impressive than the first one.

About an hour later, ten utterly stunning paintings had been produced.

The poor guy looked absolutely wiped out! He disappeared for a well-earned lie-down, I should think. The rest of us filed up to the front to inspect his handiwork.

Being my usual sceptical self, I took my time examining the paintings, but the detail was even *more* impressive close-up. What struck me the most was the uniqueness of each picture. It was as if ten separate artists had painted them, which I suppose they had! The final picture he'd painted was a portrait of a beautiful Victorian lady, and was so amazingly lovely.

Apparently – and you'll have to forgive my lack of knowledge on this subject – people were saying that what he'd done was simply impossible because the oil paints he'd used needed to dry before detail could be added. It should've take hours to do *one* painting. He'd managed ten masterpieces (in my humble opinion) in just one short hour!

Then came the auction. The paintings were to be sold, and the money raised would be used back in Brazil to help a variety of worthy causes.

This amazing man, who'd had no artistic training, didn't take one penny from the hundreds and thousands he'd raised over the years. He'd used much of it to set up a centre that'd helped countless adults and children from his country.

The auction was a real surprise. Vince and I sat with our eyes bulging while people's bids got higher and higher. I thought the paintings would go for maybe seventy, eighty quid, max. I even had an idea I might try and nab one myself, for my reading room at home, as apparently the paintings exuded healing abilities. But within minutes figures of hundreds of pounds were being casually thrown out.

I did attempt to bid for one, an abstract painting, which no one particularly seemed to like, but I pulled out when it got to seventy pounds. Also, I noticed that a really sweet elderly lady seemed to be quite desperate to secure it.

In the end the bidding rose to about two hundred and fifty pounds, much less than the others, and the other bidder, a Danish gentleman, pulled out to let her have it. It was so touching when we all had a quick whip-round and raised most of the money for her. It was such a wonderful moment; you had to be there to appreciate the intense love in that room. (Sorry to sound like a hippie. Peace, man, and all that!)

The star of the day was the Victorian lady, who went for over five hundred pounds! I swear she had a slightly smug look on her face as her chuffed-to-bits new owner, a friend of mine called John, proudly carried her off to his room.

The time between November '06 and January '07 is a little bit of a blur, because over this time Gina was poorly, although of course at the time we didn't realise quite *how* poorly!

I do remember attending a short weekend mediumship course in the December. A lovely tutor called Sandra, who coincidentally also lives in Bognor, told me (for some bizarre reason) that she conducted spiritual funerals. Handing me her card, she said comfortingly; 'You never know, you might need my services one day!'

I thanked her and said I'd keep it in mind. Then promptly threw it in the nearest bin! I suppose no one likes to think of things like funerals, and mediums are no exception.

In the last few days of Gina's life I made a promise to my spirit friends. If they took extremely good care of her over there, I would do *everything* in my power to...

A) Help as many people as I could in their grief at losing a loved one.

B) Share with as many as possible the simple but wonderful truth that we ALL survive physical death.

The first promise was relatively simple to keep. I just carried on with my private readings. I was hardly doing hundreds – maybe around thirty a month. In truth, I could've done as many as I wanted, as the demand was there. But I've always believed in quality rather that quantity, and I get too tired if I overdo it. I think people deserve to have a good hour or so spent on them. I know some readers who try and pack in as many as possible in a week, and good luck to them. But I can't – not if I'm to do a thorough and proper job.

My spirit-team understands that around thirty a month is my max, and they're fine with this number. So I feel I'm fulfilling my first promise.

The second part of the promise regarding sharing the fact that we all survive death is slightly more difficult.

Although I get so excited about the spiritual realms, and all the wonderful evidence I've personally received, I don't think it's fair to expect it to be everyone's cup of char.

I get quite upset when other people try and convince me that THEIR way of thinking is the RIGHT way, whether it's a certain religion, or an atheist who's adamant that when we die, we die! I wanted to reach those who had an interest in spiritual matters (not necessary religion) and who were seeking answers.

There was no way I was about to start touring the country, demonstrating my abilities to huge audiences... far too nerve-wracking! So a book seemed to be the perfect answer for me to keep my promise. I could share my personal experiences with people that were interested, then, combined with any experiences they'd had, they could make up their own mind to the reality of the spiritual realms.

I will do my best to fulfil these two promises I made the final days before Gina 'went home'. I realise that if I don't keep up my end of the bargain, Gina's hardly going to be neglected Up There, but a promise is a promise!

Another mediumship course I attended shortly after Gina's passing was pretty uneventful – apart from one thing that I would really like to share with you...

On the course there was an American lady in her thirties called Molly. When she insisted that everyone call her 'Morning Star' instead of Molly, a lot of people suddenly caught 'rolling-eyes-syndrome'.

In the first class I freely admit that I wasn't too happy when the tutor decided to pair me off with 'Morning Star'. We sat opposite each other and started the exercise, which was attempting to interpret each other's aura. In all honesty, it was pretty basic, flowery stuff that we were both coming out with, but what surprised me the most was how well we were getting on together. She seemed such an outgoing confident person, but not in an obnoxious way. I'd expected her to be a bit of a Spiritual-Diva. I've met a fair few of *those* in my time. Once again I'd pre-judged someone just because they'd wanted to be called an unusual name. (When will I learn?)

Over the course of the week, I didn't see Morning Star very much, but on the last evening in the bar she came over to me and pressed something into my hands. It was the beautiful silver starfish necklace she'd been wearing all week, which had been admired by all.

'I want you to have this, Anne.'

I was totally gobsmacked. Why was she giving away her gorgeous necklace? And to me – someone she hardly knew!

'I've worn it for years,' Morning Star told me. 'But when

I was in the shower this evening it fell off and for some reason I got a picture of you in my mind. Then I knew I had to pass it on to you.'

She then began to tell me the story behind the starfish necklace.

'I was out on the ocean with friends and they were all jumping in having a great time, snorkelling. One by one they came back to the boat and told me about the incredible starfish they'd seen on the reef, and that I should go and take a look. But I didn't have the confidence and was too scared to try. Afterwards, I regretted not doing it, and when I saw this starfish necklace I bought it, and have worn it ever since. It reminds me not to let opportunities pass me by just because of fear. You wear it, Anne. It'll bring you confidence, and help you manage your fears.'

Morning Star, if you are reading this, I DO wear it, almost every day, and it really *does* help.

I don't particularly believe that certain objects hold 'special powers', but the starfish necklace, too me, is magical, because I know that it meant a lot to Morning Star, and she gave it to me! She must've sensed what I so desperately try to hide... my insecurities and fears.

17

Haunted House In Herefordshire

For Christmas, Andy and I were invited to my brother Rick and his partner, Carol's house in Herefordshire. My mum, Steve, and a close family friend, another Anne, also joined us.

It had been a very painful and sad year for us all. Apart from losing Gina, a very close family friend's daughter had been killed in a car accident. She was only in her twenties. Then, to top the year off nicely, Andy's Dad, my wonderful father-in-law, Jim, passed away at the end of November.

So it's fair to say that we were all looking forward to spending a few days together, chilling out with a few glasses of mulled wine, or in Mum's case sherry. I was also looking forward to playing our beloved board games, whilst watching Steve a.k.a. The Stomach stuff his face with Carol's home-made mince pies and as many Quality Streets as humanly possible.

Another reason I was immensely looking forward to finally visiting this particular house was because, according to Rick, and quite a few other people, it was haunted!

My work as a medium has taken me into many private houses, and lots of the occupants have told me they think their place *might* be haunted. I've personally not yet come across a *real* haunted house. Honrad had told me on the flight back from Denmark that there are a *few* spirit people who refuse to leave when they pass over. But he'd stressed to me that this was exceptionally rare, and they didn't stay around for long if they did chose the 'hanging-around' option.

So with that in mind, I wasn't expecting a great deal to happen...

I love spending time with my big brother Rick. He's a really incredible individual, and he's also very talented.

As well as being a qualified Yoga teacher, he's an amazing composer and has written and produced some wonderful pieces of music, mostly classical and jazz.

Rick's what I call a philosopher. Whereas Steve is 'The Stomach', Rick is 'The Thinker'. I always really enjoy the chats we have about spiritual things. He's also a fantastic psychic and healer, but like many of us doing this kind of work, he lacks confidence in his natural abilities.

His partner, Carol, is also a very sensitive person, and both of them are strict vegetarians. I love my meat, but Rick has never preached at me or anyone else to change their eating habits, as I'm ashamed to say *I* did when I was a vegetarian for seven years.

All the way up to Herefordshire I teased Andy that he might even get to see a real live ghoulie at last. (Well, as live as a ghost *can* be!)

'It's quite a size!' was Andy's only comment as we pulled up onto the driveway.

Don't get Andy wrong – we're not talking about Buckingham Palace here! But compared to your average semi it *was* pretty impressive.

We both stared at the huge whitewashed house, with its pretty light green porch. Rick had informed me that it'd been built sometime in the sixteenth century. It had secret rooms and everything.

As cliché as it sounds, a freezing shiver rippled right down my spine as I entered the house. I glanced at Andy, but as he was hidden under the huge pile of Christmas goodies he was carrying in from the car, I couldn't gage his reaction.

Inside, sitting cosily in front of the roaring open fire, armed with a mug of tea and a slice of Carol's delicious Christmas cake, the shivery sensations I'd experienced earlier seemed to fade to nothing.

Anyway, I prided myself on the fact that it would take a hell of a lot to scare *me* after all the things I'd witnessed over the years.

Just as I was starting to switch off and relax, the inevitable question was thrown my way. (Happens every time – hazard of the job!)

The questioner was Carol. 'Are you picking up anything here, Anne? What can you sense?'

I smiled politely. 'Nothing much at the moment.'

Carol glanced over at my brother. 'Did Rick tell you about that figure we both saw a few weeks ago?'

Rick nodded. 'Yes, that was extremely odd.'

Steve comically rolled his eyes. 'Can't wait to hear the next instalment of *The Addams Family*!'

Ignoring him, the rest of us made encouraging noises, wanting to find out what had happened.

'Well, we were sitting here one evening when we both noticed a small ball of what we thought was smoke coming out of the fire. As we watched the ball built up slowly into a distinct full-height figure of a person. It just stood there while we stared at it, then it disappeared. It was just the strangest thing.'

Carol nodded in agreement. 'I've never seen anything like it.'

I know my brother and he never exaggerates or tells fairy-stories just for effect. If he saw something he would report it exactly as it happened.

'Two for one offer at Specsavers this month!' Steve quipped. But all the same I noticed he'd put down his slice of cake, looking a little uneasy.

Intrigued, I asked if Rick had any other spooky stories to share with us.

Rick laughed. 'Yes, quite a few; I could probably fill a book. I think the two strangest things that have ever happened to me involved a deer and a clock.'

Faint mutterings that sounded suspiciously like the theme tune to '*The Twilight Zone*' wafted over from where Steve was sitting, an innocent expression on his face.

'The first incident happened a few years ago, when I

was riding home on my motorbike. A deer shot straight out in front of me. It just appeared from nowhere. There was no way I could avoid it, so I braced for impact. But this is the crazy bit,' Rick told us. 'I just drove straight through it. I could see it but it wasn't there! I thought maybe I'd hallucinated it or something, so I turned back to see what'd happened.'

By this point I noticed that even Steve's ears were twitching away as he sat there pretended to read a newspaper.

'But the deer *was* real,' Rick said. 'There it was, laying stone dead by the side of the road.'

'What had happened then?' I asked, puzzled by the ending of the story.

Rick shrugged. 'I don't know, but I think my guardian angel must've been looking after me that day.'

Andy, who'd been listening intently, suddenly piped up, 'I think it could've been the deer's *spirit* you saw. That's why you were able to pass straight through it! You didn't notice the dead body because you were focused on the *spirit* of the deer.'

Rick looked quite astounded at Andy's simple, but obvious, explanation. 'I never even thought of that! You could be right, Andy.'

'Yes, animals also have souls, Steve,' I said, catching his dubious glances. 'I've had loads of pets wanting to make contact with their human friends.'

'The other thing with the clock was just as weird,' Rick – now on a roll – told his captivated audience.

Glancing over at Steve, I could almost see the thought-bubble over his head saying, '*No more! Please have mercy*!'

Mum nodded. 'Yes, I was there when that happened.'

'I'd lost the little travelling clock I use for my yoga classes. It just completely vanished one day. About a week later, I was standing in the spare bedroom at Mum's bungalow, and said out loud in frustration: "Where's my clock gone?"

That *second*, it fell out of nowhere and landed by my feet!'

I, of course, know the room, and there's only a bed and bedside table in there, so it couldn't have toppled off anything. I'd actually heard this story before, as Mum had told me it. She'd said that at first Rick had accused *her* of chucking the clock at him – which of course she hadn't.

I suppose there could be some sort of rational explanation – can't think what – but Rick thinks his spirit mates were having a few fun and games with him.

Over the years, I've heard quite a few clock-themed stories. They do seem to like playing with time!

I really enjoyed hearing Rick's paranormal stories. I wish *so much* that I'd recorded all the incredible stories my clients have confided in me. It has been *such* a massive privilege to hear all their unique experiences.

Upstairs, Andy and I were very impressed with our huge bedroom, with its en-suite that was about the same size of our bedroom at home.

I couldn't help but wonder if I would have any of my usual 'visitors' in the night. But it turned out to be quite an uneventful one – for me, anyway!

Not so for Steve!

It's quite ironic that Mr Sceptical Steve was the one to see a ghost that night.

Since Gina's passing in the January, Steve had had quite a few spiritual experiences, including the reading and meditation we did with him. Now he had his Very First Ghost (ahh, bless) to add to his growing psychic c.v.

I'll never forget his amazed face as he relayed the night's events to us.

'I woke up and there was this old lady walking – well gliding – across the room. She totally ignored me as I yelled at her. Then she disappeared through the wall.'

At first we thought he was winding us up, but after a while it was obvious he was telling the truth. He swore on Gina's grave that he'd really seen the old lady, and there's

NO WAY ON EARTH he would've done that if he was just making it up. Also, at some point he would've burst out laughing and admitted to us that he was just having a bit of fun, but to this day he insists he saw this woman as clear as anything.

Later that day, after Christmas dinner, I was alone upstairs in the bedroom. Everyone else was downstairs in the living-room, which was quite a way from my bedroom. I'd just popped up to grab a jumper. Quite clearly I heard what sounded like two little girls singing *O Come All Ye Faithful!*

What the...

I rushed out into the hall. The singing was coming from the attic rooms. I must admit, I felt quite nervous as I climbed the stairs to find the source of the mysterious carol singing. I was pretty sure I'd left everyone downstairs, and I knew no one else was in the house, certainly no children.

'Hello! Anyone there?'

No reply.

There were three rooms on the third floor, and after a good nose about I came to the obvious conclusion that they were all completely deserted.

Very strange. The singing was definitely objective, and not just in my head.

Shivering, I ran back down to the others and asked if they'd played any carols whilst I'd been upstairs. But no, they'd been chatting and clearing up the dinner things.

Of course I told them all about it. Steve turned a little green. He looked about ready to pack up and go home. All this spooky stuff just wasn't his cup of tea at all. He made some feeble joke about Carol probably putting a bit too much sherry in the trifle.

Rick looked thoughtful. 'I've heard quite a lot of children in this house, playing and chatting together. I don't think they're ghosts, just spirit children having fun.'

'Oh, that's all right then!' Steve said sarcastically. 'No ghosts, *only* spirits!'

Rick grinned at Steve. 'Don't worry, there's plenty of ghosts as well. Like the old lady you saw last night. She's on a loop!'

Steve nearly choked on his mulled wine. 'Loop. What loop?'

'Oh, she's been seen before. We think she's like an old recording that keeps playing over and over. There's no intelligence there, so no need to get upset if you see her again.'

Steve's poor face! In the end Mum had to swap rooms with him. After all, *she* was *used* to seeing strange people wandering about aimlessly all night long.

What a palaver!

Interestingly, Steve had another psychic-episode recently, when he came to stay for a weekend with me and Andy.

Steve was in a great mood because he'd met a lady called Jackie for the first time that day. They'd been emailing for a few weeks, and now had finally met up in the flesh. According to Steve, they'd hit it off really well. Since Gina's passing although Steve had had a couple of relationships, they'd all fizzled out. So we were all pleased for him.

While we ate our breakfast on the Sunday morning, Steve told us that in the night he'd had the shock of his life. He'd seen a lady sitting on our sofa looking at him intently as he lay on our old inflatable bed.

I instinctively knew that the lady was linked to Jackie, and was 'checking out' Steve.

A few days later, Steve saw Jackie for another date and described the lady he'd seen in my house. Jackie confirmed that her mum had passed away a year ago, and his description matched perfectly.

They naturally got on to the subject of spiritual things, and Jackie told Steve she'd had a brilliant reading (her words) about four years ago with a youngish psychic with long blonde hair. She said she couldn't remember the name of the lady, but the medium's husband had driven her up from the south coast.

Steve told me that as he sat there sipping his pint, huge bells started clanging in his head.

Ding-dong!

'My God, I think it might've been my *sister*!'

Jackie couldn't believe it, but searching through my old comments books there was her name and comment in black and white; *Amazing reading! Very good. Thank you.*

Steve couldn't get over the fact I'd read for his new girlfriend four years before he'd met her. The three of us live miles apart, and the chances of this happening are pretty remote.

I know people say there's no such thing as coincidence. Whether that's true or not is debatable, but in this case I think Spirit must've had a bit of a hand in their meeting...

After Christmas, I was back at the college on yet another trance course. The highlight of the week was when the tutors 'did their thing' and went into trance on the last evening.

I'd been attending the same course for the last couple of years, and was familiar with the routine by this point. Near the end of the evening, the entranced tutors, blending with their array of various guides, would invite questions from the enthralled students.

All evening I'd been slowly gathering up the courage to ask a particular question. At first four or five hands went up, so I left it. But after that no one seemed to have a question, so I went for it...

'Can I ask something, please?' I asked timidly.

The tutor, eyes still closed, turned to me. 'Of course. Ask away, dear.'

'Do flowers have souls?'

Looking back, thinking about all the deep philosophical

and important, spiritual questions I could've asked… Like, what is the true meaning of life in the physical body? Or, could you explain in detail what God-consciousness is… and I had to go and ask something like 'Do flowers have souls?'

Maybe that's why I got such a curt answer thrown back at me.

'My dear child, flowers have *seeds*, not *souls*!'

Everyone seemed to think that this was absolutely hilarious, because they all burst out laughing. Of course, I joined in, chuckling alongside them. But inside I felt so flipping stupid.

Was it such a daft question to ask? As living organisms, I felt sure that flowers would have some sort of soul-energy. I realise of course that it wouldn't be the same as a human soul – it could be more evolved for all we knew!

I'd read somewhere about certain tests that'd been done on plants and flowers where they'd reacted negatively to things like pairs of scissors coming towards them. (Who wouldn't react negatively to a long shiny pair of scissors heading their way? I do – just ask my hairdresser!) Flowers also respond really positively to plenty of love and attention. Hence my question whether they have some sort of soul.

I have no interest whatsoever in gardens or gardening, and hardly know the difference between a plant and a weed. Strange really, seeing I'm a professional gardener's daughter. So I don't know why this question has always intrigued me. I think it's because the plant kingdom is a bit of a grey area, spiritually-speaking. People can stretch to animals surviving death, well, as long as they're cute and cuddly, but that's a discussion for another day!

But plants? Well, why not?

So stop eating that poor carrot immediately! It has a soul!

Only kidding. But it's food for thought, though, isn't it?

18

Our Psychic Workshop

The year was whizzing by. It was already March, and I'd just reached my ninth anniversary as a professional reader. People kept reminding me of another big date – it was my fortieth in November. (As if I was likely to forget *that* little fact!)

Nine whole years! What a roller coaster of a journey it'd been! All those people I'd been privileged enough to meet along the way.

All those readings...

In truth, I have a real love/hate thing going on with my readings.

I DO love it. It's my life. But there's no way round it; it does provoke a lot of negative emotions in me, too.

However much specific evidence I obtain, I *always* think I should've got more. My clients can be hugging and thanking me profusely, and I can still be thinking; *Why didn't I get her mum's name, or birthday, or whatever?*

You can also end up feeling quite bruised and battered after a reading. Being sandwiched between the client and spirit's intense emotions is, frankly, pretty exhausting.

Then there's all the anxiety and nerves I feel before every reading. Sometimes the nerves can be so overwhelming, and quite difficult to cope with. It's silly really. It's not as if I'm about to be thrown into an arena with a dozen hungry lions. (Although with one or two clients I've had it might be marginally preferable!)

It's something I've had to learn to control and live with. I've also suffered from quite a few panic attacks whilst Andy has driven me to psychic parties at various houses. I DO NOT recommend them.

I can just see budding mediums reading this and thinking, '*Oh God, maybe it's not worth it. I'll stick to something less stressful like bomb disposal!'*

Please don't let my words put you off. Everyone's journey is unique to them. Yes, it *will* be bloody hard work. It *will* be painful, frustrating, tiring, nerve-racking, and sometimes utterly heart breaking, hearing and being a part of people's tragic stories.

But there's also the most incredible feeling that's so hard to describe, when there's a real live spirit person working alongside you. You are part of a wonderful team, and together you will do your best to help the person that's come to see you – the medium – to reach their loved-ones. You can touch them in such a positive way it could potentially change their way of thinking and their lives forever. What could be cooler than that?

In my first year of reading, I asked Honrad what I needed to be a great medium. Grabbing a pen and paper, I scribbled down the answers I was lucky enough to receive.

1. *Have an open compassionate heart that doesn't judge*

2. Have patience

3. *Have big ears*

Big ears? My ears are quite small and dainty, thank you very much, Honrad!

Oh, right. Yes. Sorry. I get it; I need to *listen*.

Using the second and third piece of advice, I waited *patiently, listening* for any other words of wisdom that might be headed my way. Some fabulous key-word that would open the chamber of my psychic abilities and allow all the information I needed to be on tap for me! If Honrad had suggested meditating on top of a snow-tipped mountain for eight hours a day, I think I would've done it. (Possibly!)

There must be something I can do, I remember thinking. *Some quick fix to 'Evidence Heaven'*!

Your psychic abilities will grow stronger and develop over time. Don't worry so much about them. Just focus on developing these three traits.

So I have. Admittedly not always as successful as I

would've liked, but I'll keep trying my best. It's not always easy.

Many people over the years have asked me whether I do any kind of teaching, or run any psychic workshops. I didn't. But after a long chat with my friend Vince, we decided we'd give it a go.

It's something I would never in a billion years have attempted on my own, but Vince has this way of convincing me that I'm much more capable than I think I am. (It's wonderful having friends that believe in you!)

The workshop was aimed at beginners, and would consist of around fifteen to twenty of my regular clients. We wanted to incorporate a variety of exercises for the students to try-out, ranging from psychometry, mediation, basic healing and, of course, mediumship. Vince had run previous workshops, whereas this was my first, so his experience was invaluable.

To say I was a bit nervous the morning of the workshop is like saying a baby Blue Whale is a tad on the heavy side.

Vince arrived to pick me up, full of the joys of spring. Which incidentally it was – April, to be precise.

We'd booked a nice little hall near Guildford. My brother Rick had recommended it, as he used to hire it for his yoga classes.

'Are you okay?' Vince asked me, as we unloaded all our paraphernalia for the day. 'You look a bit pale.'

I waved a dismissive hand. 'I'm fine. Can't wait to get started.'

Inside we set up the tea and coffee things. Vince had even brought a huge tin of biscuits, which I knew would go down a treat.

As we set up the room, we discussed the itinerary for the day. Vince wanted to 'go with the flow', whereas I wanted to stick rigidly to the exercises we'd planned, so there was a little tension between us, but we soon sorted it out.

Spotting an old piano in the corner of the hall, I decided

to try and raise the energy by plonking out a very bad rendition of *Greensleeves.*

At least it impressed Vince. He wasn't aware that I could play the piano. (I'm a lady of many hidden talents!) My granddad McKay taught me to bash out a few tunes. Unfortunately, *Greensleeves* and *When The Red, Red, Robin Comes Bob Bob-Bobbin' Along,* is about my portfolio. (Granddad didn't do any post-war songs!)

I was just contemplating on treating Vince to my version of *Red, Red Robin,* when lucky for him the first people started to arrive, complete with their packed lunches.

Ten minutes later and I couldn't believe how many people had turned up. There were twenty in total. They were aware of the fact they were being our 'guinea pigs' and everyone seemed really psyched-up to be a part of the day.

We sat them in a semi-circle, and after the chatter had died down, I said hello, introduced Vince, and thanked them all for coming along. Then my mind went utterly blank. I couldn't take all those eyes staring expectantly at me.

I had planned what to say after the introductions, but my tongue just refused to co-operate with my brain.

Thankfully, Vince stepped in, and between us we explained the day we had organised for them.

After a short 'opening up' exercise, I handed out envelops. Inside, were pictures we'd cut out of magazines of famous people. Some were deceased, like Elizabeth 1st and Einstein, and some still very much alive and kicking, such as Simon Cowell and Madonna.

I knew that most of our eager students were pretty much virgins when it came to all this sort of psychic-stuff, so I was a little on the nervous side about this particular exercise. It was quite a difficult one for beginners.

Oh ye of little faith!

That did *fantastically* well! Apart from one lady, who picked up a wonderful, gentle, kindly person in her envelope – it was Adolf Hitler! We all had a good old laugh at that one.

They'd all managed to pick up pretty accurate information on their famous person. Vince and I were extremely impressed. A guy who'd been (in his words) 'dragged here under protest' by his partner, didn't really seem to be very impressed with anything. He held his 'mystery-person' envelope and blurted out, 'It's Elvis!'

Imagine the uproar there was when he opened his envelope and Elvis Presley *did* pop out! (Not in person, obviously – now that *really* would've been something!)

Next, we got them to place something they owned, such as a piece of jewellery, on a tray, and covered it with a piece of cloth. They each had a 'lucky-dip' under the cloth and took something off the tray to work with.

I know that psychometry works, but I *still* believe our hard-working guides are working alongside us as we are holding the object in question, impressing us with the relevant information, *rather* than the information coming from the object per se! But I know other sensitives have different opinions on this subject.

Once again they picked up specifics on each other's lives, including information on their children, health, work, even pets they owned. One or two started to pick up some relevant names, and Vince and I realised that spirit people were trying to make links with them.

In the lunch break, as it was such a lovely day, everyone sat outside on the grass with their packed lunches.

After lunch, Vince took them on a brilliant meditation to meet their personal guides. He's got such a fantastic tone of voice that everyone drifted off quickly into his or her own private world. I observed each of them in turn and tuned in to who was drawing close to them. After, I went through who I'd sensed with them. For some it was a relative, but for the majority, it was their guide. It was quite mind-blowing to witness all those evolved souls standing proudly by their charges as they took their first baby steps on his or her unique spiritual journey.

Over the years, I've had many hundreds of people ask me who their guides are, and it's a question that always makes me groan inside. Guides are *such* a personal thing.

In the past, I've asked this question myself to many psychics, and have been given all sorts of confusing and contradicting answers. My clients have also told me of some 'weird and wonderful' guides working alongside them. One lady told me she'd paid the hefty sum of sixty-five pounds to be informed she had a 'Golden Unicorn' guiding her on her earthly journey.

I asked this lady if she had an affinity with unicorns, thinking that it could be symbolic and meaningful to her, but no, she didn't know anything about unicorns. (She didn't even particularly like horses!) I don't want to disrespect someone else's work, but putting it bluntly, in my opinion, this was a load of old cobblers! I assured her I could clearly see her REAL guide standing by her side, and it was most definitely not a Golden Unicorn – it was a Pink Elephant! I'm only kidding, of course. No, I couldn't see any particular guide with her, but I *did* pick up good, solid evidence from her loved-ones.

The frustrating thing about picking up on guides is that they, of course, can't be proven. The best you can hope for is to pick up on the same guide that a previous psychic has, which gives it more credibility. Unfortunately, even that has its flaws, as most seem to have been given Native Americans, Chinese philosophers, or nuns. I'm not saying these people *aren't* guides, but surely there must be millions of other souls that don't fit into these categories who also guide us? Don't *they* get a look in?

The other thing I've noticed about guides is that some people, even a few mediums I've met, tend to almost worship them. I might be on shaky ground here, but my personal belief is that worshipping anything is a very unhealthy occupation. Admire – yes. Worship – no!

Any evolved soul would definitely discourage any sort of hero-worshipping. They are there to work alongside us, and to inspire us to be the best that we can be. They are our colleges and our friends. They are evolving spiritually just as we are, and they will make mistakes occasionally, just as we do. The last thing they want is to be plonked on a pedestal and worshipped.

After the meditation, Vince took the group through a very basic lesson in healing, which everyone seemed to thoroughly enjoy.

I've administered healing a few times over the years, but it's definitely not my field of expertise. From crystal to chakra, angel therapy to good old Reiki, the list of different types of healing is endless.

I truly believe whatever tools the healer is using, the *most important* thing is their *intent*.

Thought is *such* a *powerful* energy. If the healer is thinking about what they're cooking for the kid's tea, or who's having an affair with whom in their favourite soap opera, the healing is not going to be very effective. But if they are pouring all his or her love and compassion into the person they're healing, whatever method is being used, it will have a much higher chance of being successful. The healer needs to visualise their patient's various health problems being surrounded in healing energy – and that takes a lot of intense concentration.

From what I've observed, there seems to be a little too much emphasis on the tools being used, *rather* than the healer's natural compassion.

I must add here that when it comes to healing I do believe there is an exception in just having 'good intent'. There is a branch of healing known as *'Psychic Surgery'* which is an extremely rare form of *physical* mediumship. I don't really understand much about this, but I know that my friend Vince has 'sat' for many years developing the correct energy-blend which allows him to practise this unique form of healing. I know he has achieved some truly stunning results, and people's lives have changed dramatically after they've consulted him. My nan used to say 'the proof is in the pudding', and I think that old proverb is very apt here. If miraculous results are being achieved, then something fantastic is going on!

Unfortunately, I think people are quite sceptical of this sort of healing because so very little is known about it.

I once watched a clip of a psychic-operation. The 'surgeon's' hands were kneading away at this poor lady's tummy like she was a lump of dough, and there was what I assumed was 'blood' all over the place. (Tomato ketchup, more likely!) It looked totally fake, especially when a piece of liver – which looked like it would be quite tasty fried up with a few onions – was triumphantly 'pulled out' from the woman's abdomen.

Interestingly, just about every personal reading I've ever had healing has been mentioned – but *not* mediumship. I must admit, I find that a bit strange.

If I'd listened to the many psychics I consulted in my twenties, I would probably be a healer right now, rather than a medium, but luckily I exercised my free will and went down the mediumship path – which I know without a doubt was the right one.

After our healing session, we paired everyone off and asked one to be the medium and one the recipient. This is where the hard work *really* started.

The truth about mediumship is that it's extremely tricky to teach. In fact, all you can really do is guide someone through the process, then encourage them to trust the information they're receiving so they can pass it on to the recipient.

The various mediumship courses I've attended over the years have often stressed the importance of 'passing on what you get' – no more, no less. Some teachers have even told me that you should never ask for additional information, but why not?

Spirit can get as flustered and emotionally overwhelmed as we do when a reading is in progress. Occasionally, all his or her carefully prepared 'evidence' and 'messages' can fly out the provable window when they attempt to communicate through the medium.

To some extent I agree that it's very important to pass on exactly what you get, *but* I've also discovered you need to ASK the spirit person as much as you can. Be nosy. You're looking for pure twenty-four carat gold evidence. So dig, dig, dig, then take that metaphorical shovel and dig some more. It's so important for the new up-and-coming generation of mediums to push the boundaries like never before. The only limits are the ones we set ourselves.

Imagine you are interviewing the spirit person. Ask them...

'What's your name?'

'How did you pass?'

'What did you do for a living?'

'How many children have you got?'

'What are their names?'

'What do they do?'

'Did you have any pets? What were their names?'

The list is of course endless...

You need to really get to know the spirit trying to communicate, and chat to them as if he or she was a real live person – which of course they *are*.

The answers may come in the form of words, pictures, feelings, even smells, or a combination of all these elements. Sometimes it's just a 'knowing' which is hard to convey. It's like the information just slips off your tongue.

So, as we circled our ten pairs of students, we encouraged them to ask their spirit people questions. Keeping in mind that almost all them had never had a link in their lives, they were coming out with relevant evidence that was pretty impressive. Yes, there were holes in the information, but that was to be expected. With a bit of time and practice, it was clear that many of them had the makings of good solid mediums.

For the final half-hour of the day, we had a questions-and-answers session scheduled.

I'd been dreading this bit, worried a query would be fired at me that I couldn't answer. I felt comforted that Vince was sitting by my side. His span of knowledge and wisdom regarding the psychic-world is greater than just about anyone I've ever met.

One of the students expressed her amazement that she'd managed to achieve such a good link with a spirit person. She told us she'd always thought mediums were born, so wondered how she'd done it.

Very interesting question! Vince and I both agreed on this one.

Some people are born with strong natural mediumship ability, *but* even if someone's not blessed in this way, it *is* possible, with a high degree of dedicated practice, to become an extremely skilled medium. It's just the same as any other ability really.

In my time, I've known a few 'natural' mediums who've become quite lazy and complacent with their links – they just haven't pushed themselves, and it ends up showing in the quality of their survival evidence. But on the other hand, I've also know mediums who aren't what you'd call 'natural-born' but give their all. Consequently, they're absolutely fantastic!

I firmly believe spirit people will work with anyone who genuinely wants to help others and make a difference.

The other question that was asked at our workshop was, 'How can you tell your own thoughts from spirits?'

This is a tricky one. It's my belief it's one of – if not *the* biggest – obstacle in mediumship.

I've seen it so many times. A link starts off so promising, then good old imagination kicks in and the link is lost.

Spirit people are constantly fighting to get their information across. The link is as fragile as a spider's web, and if it breaks the medium's mind will obligingly jump-in to fill the gaps. You can only be aware that this *might* happen.

If 'No's' are coming at you thick and fast, then you've probably lost the link. You need to clear your mind, go back, and try and re-establish it as fast as possible. Same as anything worthwhile, it takes time and practise – that's all.

Everyone left our workshop with a great big smile on their faces, so we took that as a sign they'd enjoyed their day with us. (Unless they were grinning because their ordeal was finally over!)

The feedback we got the following week was amazing. We even received some thank-you cards. Everyone seemed eager to attend any other workshops that we might arrange in the future.

On a personal level, I felt like I'd finally taken a huge step forward in overcoming my fear of talking in front of an audience. I knew (and still know) I've got a long way to go, but it's so true what they say; the first steps are the hardest.

That night, I had a massive thumbs up from Honrad and the gang. They were more than happy with the workshop, thank goodness!

The following month, I met a young lady called Mel, and once again my spiritual life took an unexpected turn.

19

Let's Get Physical!

Mel came to see me for a private reading. The only thing I can remember about Mel's reading was her grandmother making an appearance and telling me that Mel had mended a puncture on a paddling pool the previous day, which Mel understood. Apart from that, I just remember it went pretty well. Mel's one of those people who are incredibly easy and enjoyable to read for.

Aspects of Mel's own psychic abilities had surfaced briefly in the course of the reading, so I already knew she'd had quite a lot of experience with psychic stuff. After the reading, she said she wanted a chat. So I made us a cuppa, intrigued to know what she wanted to talk about...

'Would you be interested in sitting in a physical mediumship circle?' Mel asked, sipping her tea.

Whatever I was expecting, it wasn't that!

The only previous experience I'd had of physical mediumship was the table-tilting we'd done on the paranormal course I'd attended. As I explained before, the photos I've seen of physical mediumship being demonstrated, looked, to my eyes, so obviously faked, I'd not even considered it.

Vince has always had a very strong draw to physical mediumship, especially the psychic surgery, and we've spent many happy hours chin-wagging on the phone about it. But apart from the insight I'd gained from our chats, it was all new territory to me. I only needed to hear the word 'ectoplasm' to start feeling queasy.

Mel explained that she and a few others had sat in a physical circle for about seven years, but it'd abruptly come to an end when their medium had had to pull out, for some reason or another. Mel wanted me to be the new medium.

The only thing I *did* know about physical mediumship – from my chats with Vince, and the little bit I'd researched myself – was that to do it properly it took *many* years to develop.

It was true that table-tilting, and things flying about the room, *could* be achieved quite quickly, but the *real meaningful* stuff takes time – lots of time!

I'm talking about stuff such as materialisation – spirit people appearing via ectoplasm. Apports – such as Vince's gifts at the dinner table. And direct-voices – not just a medium in trance, but real spirit people talking!

Materialisation is about a rare as a scientist taking a medium's work seriously. (Only kidding – please don't sue!) I've only ever met one person who has actually witnessed full materialisation, and she was a very well respected medium and teacher herself. But apart from her, it always seems to be a friend of a friend's cousin's next-door-neighbour, who saw it in 1962... or something along those lines.

The other thing – apart from its elusive nature – that I've always disliked about physical, is the fact it all seems to take place in pitch-black conditions, which makes me (and the sceptics, I'm sure) feel more than a little suspicious. People's imaginations can so easily go into over-drive in 'dark and spooky' surroundings.

So taking everything into account, I'm not quite sure why I agreed to give it a go. I think that perhaps the chats I'd had with my friend Vince had influenced me more strongly than I'd realised.

To begin with, we had quite a few problems with our circle. The location changed three times, and people kept joining, then, for whatever reason, moving on.

A year later there were five of us left. Apart from Mel and me, there was Angela, a lovely lady in her sixties, John, a spiritual healer also in his sixties, and Mel's brother, Mark.

By this point we were using my reading room to hold the circle. We'd had special curtains made to block out any light, and Mark had even built us a cosy little canvas cabinet for me to sit in.

Our first real success happened almost exactly one year later – which is quite good for physical phenomena.

On that May evening, we had scattered rose petals randomly in the middle of the circle. After the light was snapped back on, the petals had been moved about to form the shape of a love heart. Ahh, very sweet!

No one in the group had moved the petals. It would've been impossible to grope about in the dark, undetected, in such a small room. Plus, I know that none of us would've deceived the rest of the group in that way.

We were all pretty excited about this small breakthrough.

Around September, I linked with a spirit gentleman who kept repeating he wanted us to contact a lady with butterfly tattoos, and bring her into the circle. After I obtained some more information, Mel and Mark realised who the gentleman was. It was Greg; a close friend of Mark's who'd recently taken his own life. The tattooed lady was Greg's wife, Rachel.

Through my trance mediumship, spirit told the group to bring Rachel in just before Christmas. They said that they would try their very best to apport something for her. She would provide the 'bridge of love' spirit needed to assist them in manifesting the apport.

After I came out of trance, I was quite shocked when the others excitedly told me that we'd been promised an apport. Being honest, I was aware that I had said these words during the trance-session regarding the apport, but I still felt amazed they'd come out of my mouth. I prayed Spirit could back-up their incredible promise.

Soon enough it was three days before Christmas, and we were holding our last circle of the year. As we'd agreed with spirit, Rachel had been invited along and had readily accepted – so there was a definite air of expectancy circulating the room as we settled down for the night's events.

As the medium, I prepared myself to go into the physical-state. I shut my eyes and allowed our spirit friends to draw as close as possible. The energy seemed to be building up nicely. The only way to describe it is it's like waves of electricity rippling through my body and into the room.

Each week I felt this tingly-ripply sensation to differing degrees, but tonight it was the strongest I'd ever experienced.

Rachel hadn't had much experience with anything psychic, so I hoped they evening wouldn't prove too much for her. So far, she seemed extremely comfortable with the whole scenario, but within a short amount of time, Rachel was calling out to Greg, pleading with him to join us. It was quite heart-breaking hearing the deep pain and anguish in her voice.

If ever anyone needs communication it's her, I thought as I sat there. *Surely this is what it's all about?*

As I drifted deeper into the physical-state, I was aware that Rachel was telling the others she could sense Greg standing next to her, and could feel his arms embracing her.

I've got to point out here that I realise Rachel was in a highly emotional state, so can't vouch for what she was sensing, but as a medium, I knew for sure Greg *was* in the room and *was* standing beside her.

After I came out of the physical-state, I switched to mental mediumship, and Greg passed me some extremely good evidence, including her birthday, both her grandparent's names – they wanted to say 'hi' and some very specific stuff about their life together. He told me to mention 'honey on a plate'. I didn't have a clue what this meant, but she gasped and said she'd been given this *exact sentence* a few months previous with another medium, and it was meaningful to her!

I couldn't shut Greg up! He must've rattled on for well over an hour given fact after fact. It was fantastic to be able to pass on all his wonderful evidence and messages.

I've never done a reading in pitch-black, but I would highly recommend it. No distractions – just Greg's voice and pictures in my head. It was great! Sometimes mediums can unintentionally pick up signs from people's faces, which can influence their work in a negative way, but of course darkness eliminates this problem. After this experience I was almost tempted to get myself a blindfold, but didn't think it would go down very well with my clients!

When we switched on the light, we had a very quick look round, but couldn't see anything that might've been apported by spirit. I felt a little disappointed that the 'promised apport' hadn't materialised, but Rachel seemed very happy with the evening… that was the main thing.

I was too tired to clear up, so went straight to bed. Next morning Andy and I went in to sort out the room.

'What this?' Andy asked, bending down to pick up a small object just on the edge of the rug.

Puzzled, I took it off him. It felt warm and tingly in my hands. My heart rate almost doubled in seconds. I couldn't believe what I was seeing. It was a beautiful purple toy *butterfly*!

I'd never seen it before in my life, and I knew straight away that this was the promised apport.

Andy was a little more sceptical and said that before I got too excited I needed to check with my group that it hadn't fallen out of their pockets, or anything like that. So I sent them a very rambled text and picture. Back came the responses, and no – no one had seen it before. The idea that the butterfly was somehow carried in by their shoes was also eliminated, as my group always took off their shoes in my porch.

We were all amazed and awed that our spirit-team *had* kept their promise to us, and for them to pick a purple butterfly for her was the most significant thing in the world.

We *should* have trusted them, and searched the room more thoroughly that evening, because we will now never know for certain whether it was apported in the room *whilst* we were all there, *or* during the night.

I know many people will pour doubt on this event, and that's fair enough. But I know in my deepest heart that this was a *real* apport given with love to someone who really needed it – and my opinion on that will never change.

I didn't see Rachel after that evening, but Mel assured me that she was overwhelmed with Greg's gift, and would keep it with her always.

20

Uncle Ronnie Drops By

One day Andy and I were driving back from a psychic party having a conversation about Cosmic Ordering!

Someone had given me a book on the subject and we were discussing (rather I was discussing and poor old Andy was listening) whether it could really work.

Cosmic Ordering isn't a new idea, it's just a different name for 'Creative Visualisation', or even plain old 'Positive Thinking'.

The *basic* idea is that you create in your mind an object or situation that you really want, then focus or meditate on it, picturing yourself achieving whatever it is. Then you 'send' it out to the universe. Hopefully, it *should* then materialise in your life. That's the theory, anyway.

After me droning on and on for a good hour, Andy, probably in exasperation, said to me, 'If it works prove it!'

Actually, I hadn't said it *worked*; I was just discussing the possibilities with him that it *might*. But I thought, *why not? I'll give it a go.*

To make it a little more interesting – and because my mind went blank – I asked Andy to come up with something for me to 'order'.

'Order someone interviewing you on camera about your work,' Andy challenged me.

Hmmm! I wasn't sure on that one. Wasn't it supposed to be something you really desired? I didn't particularly *want* to be interviewed. I might get all my words mixed up. But not wanting to chicken-out, I said I'd give it a go.

So I did. That night, I vividly pictured someone asking me all these questions about my work as a medium, and the camera was right there filming it all. Then I sent it out in a blue-bubble (don't ask me why blue) to the universe.

That was it. Done!

Andy laughed when I told him, but *three* days later I had an e-mail from a young guy called Robert who was at college doing Media Studies. He asked if he could film me giving an interview about my work, for a project he was doing to achieve a particular qualification.

Smug doesn't come *close* to how I felt when Andy read through the e-mail, his eyes narrowed in disbelief.

Ha! If Andy smoked I would've told him to put *that* in his pipe and smoke it!

But behind my cool 'I told you I could do it' exterior, I was *totally* gobsmacked that it had *actually* worked.

Andy tried to put it down to coincidence, and muttered that it would've happened anyway, but I'd been a medium for almost a decade by this point, and no one had *ever* asked me for an interview before then. It seems quite a huge coincidence to me that I'd created it, then it'd actually happened!

The real deep question here is... how can I use Cosmic Ordering to create myself a private Caribbean Island!

Being serious though, it *is* a fascinating subject. I wondered if Andy was right, and I *would've* got the e-mail anyway, even if I hadn't done the ordering thingy.

Even though I had this amazing experience, I'm still unsure about Cosmic Ordering. Some books I've read make it sound so ludicrously easy. If it was as easy as that, everyone would be ordering things left, right and centre. No one would have to work, because they'd just stick in their order for a million quid, or whatever floats their boat, and basically the whole of society would come crashing down.

We're all in some way looking for the easy-less-littered-with-obstacles road, but I don't believe in get-rich-quick promises and schemes; I believe in setting goals, then working hard to achieve them.

Saying that, I *do* think Cosmic Ordering works under certain conditions:

Firstly, I wasn't too bothered about the outcome of my order. I just wanted to prove it *could* work. Maybe that's why it *did* work. Also, it was an order that was, in effect, helping someone else achieve something *they* wanted. I put out the thought and the universe, in some inexplicable and beautiful way, matched us together.

I do believe 'Thought' is extremely powerful and can greatly affect our lives. I even believe 'Thought', or 'Consciousness' can affect the material world around us.

Quantum physics is starting to prove this. As I mentioned before, it's something I'm trying to get my head round, as I think a lot of the answers regarding the existence of the spiritual realms, and even other dimensions, could be unlocked if we understood in more detail this branch of science.

So come on Quantum Scientists. No pressure, guys, but we're all waiting here with bated breath!

It was two weeks before my fortieth, and I was rushing around trying to organise the finishing touches to the huge party I was throwing with my best mate Michelle, who's forty on the same day – we think!

I say 'we think' because Michelle was a Foundling. In other words she was 'found'. Basically, someone dumped baby Michelle by a load of rubbish bins – but *thank God* she was discovered before the dustmen got to her.

So, consequently, she doesn't know her *exact* day of birth. She might've been up to a couple of day's old on the date she was found, which was 17th November 1968.

I was born on 16th November.

My mum remembers Michelle's case very well, as of course it was on the national news and in all the papers. Mum had just given birth herself – to me; so it was a topic she was naturally going to be interested in. Also, Michelle was found in London, and I was born in Westminster.

Michelle's adopted brother, Martin, is very much into

psychic stuff, and a few years ago a friend of his, using a pendulum – not my favourite thing, as you know – came up with the date of 16th November as Michelle's *real* birthdate. Her original birth certificate actually does give this date, so she decided to be just like the queen and celebrate two birthdays – just to cover all angles. Fair play to her!

Anyway, back to the up-and-coming party. It was quite early in the morning and I was in the study trying to figure out how many hotel rooms I needed to book for our guests. Andy was in bed, as he was feeling a little under the weather.

When I took him in a cup of tea, I was shocked at his appearance. He looked pale and his skin had a strange waxy sheen to it.

'I'm not feeling too great,' he murmured. 'I'm feeling really light-headed and giddy, and my chest really hurts.'

My medical knowledge is very limited, but I didn't like what I was seeing and hearing. In nearly twenty years, Andy's hardly ever complained of being ill, and here he was looking like he was almost on his deathbed.

I called the NHS helpline and described the symptoms to them. They told me to call for an ambulance. So I did.

Rushing about as we waited for the ambulance, desperately trying to collect his blood-pressure medication, and bits and bobs for the hospital, I managed to fall down the stairs and hurt my toes quite badly. In fact, I'd broken two of them, but I didn't realise that at the time, and didn't have the luxury of focusing on the pain.

I'll never forget that trip to the hospital in the back of the ambulance. It wasn't like Andy was unconscious or anything, but he looked so very ill.

Andy was only forty-six, but when you work as a medium and are used to linking with hundreds of souls who've passed at young ages, it does play on your mind how quickly and easily illness can happen. No one is immune. We all tend to live under the illusion that we're invincible, when in truth we're all so very fragile.

So of course my mind went into overdrive, and I found it hard controlling my tears. I seriously thought he could be about to 'Meet his Maker'! I prayed for Honrad and my spirit friends to draw close and give him some powerful healing.

In the midst of all the drama there was a bit of a light-hearted moment when the female doctor referred to me as Andy's daughter! Andy even managed a chuckle at that one!

One of the nurses, noticing my limp and hearing about my fall down the stairs, wanted to treat my poor tootsies, but, without sounding like a martyr, I didn't want to leave Andy.

The following day, after conducting all the relevant tests and establishing that he hadn't suffered a heart attack, Andy was allowed home. After a few more tests, it turned out he'd contracted some sort of weird infection. Within a week he was more or less back to his old self – thank God!

I'd bought the most gorgeous pair of high-heeled shoes for my fortieth party, and was really determined to wear them, broken toes or not! The dress I was wearing *demanded* high-heels.

As a rule, I'm not really a shoe-person. (Yes, any men out there reading this – we DO exist!) Wearing these shoes was a big thing for me. Very shallow, I know! I was in a hell of a lot of pain with my toes, and looking down at the very pointy black thing in my hand, I wondered how on earth I was going to get them on without first anaesthetising my foot.

So I did the sensible thing. I asked for healing from my spirit friends.

Not only did I manage to wear my shoes that evening, I even achieved a little dancing. Yes, I admit it could've been partly the wine, but I truly believe Honrad and the gang helped me out as much as they could.

The healing had been *strictly* on a temporary basis, as for a good two months after my fortieth I could barely walk, let alone dance. That *proved* to me that I did get some very powerful healing that magical evening.

Sometimes it seems to me that as soon as something lovely takes place, a tragedy seems to happen as if to balance things out, because shortly after my fortieth another member of my family went home to Spirit.

My mum's brother, Uncle Ronnie suffered a heart-attack and passed away.

Uncle Ronnie was such a wonderful man. As a child, I vividly remember all the fantastic parties we had at his house with all my cousins. He and Uncle Nor were always dressing up and fooling about. He was really into amateur dramatics and was in all the local pantomimes, usually playing the lead villain, as he had such a loud raucous voice. As a child I remember wishing he was *my* dad, because he was always so jolly and such good fun.

Don't get me wrong – I loved my dad to bits, but he was a very serious, reserved man, who spent most of his life either working or in front of the telly. He wasn't what you would describe as 'the life and soul of the party'!

Three days after Uncle Ronnie's passing, he appeared to me, smiling away happily. I only saw his head and shoulders, but could see that he looked much younger than when he'd passed. Interestingly, Uncle Ronnie had been an extremely sceptical man when it came to any sort of spiritual matters, so I was totally astonished that he had returned so quickly.

A gentleman once asked me what was the point of what I did. What real value did it have? I felt quite annoyed at such a daft question.

Surely the comfort and peace of mind people get from hearing their loved ones are fine and happy is priceless? Not to mention the fact that people's minds are being opened to realms they never knew existed. To have a really specific (not stupid wishy-washy stuff) reading, can be a mind-boggling experience, and can change even the most sceptic person's way of viewing the world.

Also, spirit can provide us with information that can truly help and guide us in our everyday lives. Very occasionally, spirits advice can be invaluable to the recipient.

Recently, a lady called Christine, who I have read for a few times in the past, rang me to book another reading.

During the reading her husband stepped forward with some wonderful evidence and messages for her. I was surprised to hear from him because I knew that he'd been alive when she'd had her last reading, two years ago; I remembered he'd been sitting in the next room, watching the telly.

After the reading, Christine stood up, hugged me, and said she wanted to thank me with all her heart.

She explained that in the previous reading, I'd had a lady step forward who'd been named as her husband's mother. The lady had given me Christine's husband's name, Harry (I didn't know that was his name) and said her son needed to go to see the doctor as soon as possible.

Although Harry insisted he was fine, Christine took his mum's advice seriously, and booked him an appointment for the next day.

After tests, Harry was found to be seriously ill, and the doctor told Christine he would've died within a month or two if he hadn't been brought in for treatment. Christine confided in the doctor that a psychic had told her to seek immediate medical help, and the doctor commented that she should thank me, as I'd given him and his family something so precious... time. Nearly two years to be precise!

With that time he was able to get things in order and say his goodbyes. Christine said Harry had wanted to meet me and thank me himself, but for some reason this meeting never took place.

It's very rare that spirit pass me this sort of health-related information. When it happens I'm always so careful in the way I pass it to the recipient. The whole health-area is such a minefield for psychics, and I wouldn't recommend any medium to start trying to diagnosis clients. This was a very unusual case, but I'm so, so pleased that I *did* pass on the information from Harry's mother.

Thank you, Christine, for allowing me to include this story about your lovely hubby, Harry.

It highlights beautifully the value of the work mediums try their hardest to do.

When I heard this story from Christine, I said to my friend Vince, 'If I don't do another reading as long as I live, at least I've done a good thing there.'

He agreed!

Epilogue

It was only when I started writing this book that I really began to appreciate how incredibly mind-boggling lucky I've been with all the amazing things I've experienced in my life.

The most important thing I have learnt throughout *all* my experiences is that we are all connected by Love.

When I look into the eyes of a mother who has lost her child, or a partner who's lost their beloved life-companion – the list is endless – I know that LOVE will build the bridge between this world and the next. Love-energy will make the communication possible. Yes, this does sound like 'new-age mumbo-jumbo' but it's the truth! In my opinion, anyway.

Although I know mediumship is very important for individuals, as it gives people so much peace to know their loved ones are fine and happy, I've always been aware of the wider implications proof of an afterlife could have on everyone.

As a child, I wasn't exposed to any particular religion. Even the experiences Mum and Nan told me about were never put across in a religious context only told in a 'matter-of-fact' way.

Of course I'd heard of Heaven and Hell – eternal bliss or pain! But it'd never made much sense to my young mind. It was far too black and white.

Funny as it sounds, I've never really thought of the spirit world as having anything to do with religion.

I remember once asking Honrad about his thoughts on religion. His answer was surprisingly simple and, to my mind, quite beautiful. He told me that the highest possible religion, in his opinion, was to try and live in the moment, and to do and be the best you can within that moment.

'Too many people try and live in the Afterlife when they should be focusing on the here and now. You'll all get over here soon enough!'

To me, the spirit world is just the next step in an incredible journey we're all on. Those who have gone before us are always excited to find themselves in the next phase of life. It's only natural for people we have loved and lost to want to come back and let us know they're okay. Why wouldn't they? I know I would.

Thousands of people I've read for have told me about their own spiritual experiences, and others ask with frustration why they never seem to get anything. I'm not sure why some don't get very much. Maybe they're not ready.

Some of us come down with the *soul* purpose of *becoming* a medium, but it doesn't make us different or special to anyone else. I believe that we can all link with spirit people. It's a bit like learning a foreign language – it just takes a little time and practice to get it right.

To most people it's an interesting subject, but they haven't got the time or energy to devote to contacting Spirit – which is fair enough. So they consult a medium.

Spirit people are always finding ways to communicate with us, and sometimes they're incredibly creative in doing this. But usually it's very subtle.

When Mum was pregnant with me, she desperately wanted a baby girl. She'd already had my two brothers and wanted the third to be the daughter she'd always longed for. Nan insisted throughout the pregnancy that I was a girl, but Mum convinced herself that I was another boy!

My dad had packed her bag ready to go into the hospital, and inside he'd placed a man-sized box of Kleenex tissues.

On the morning Mum was rushed to hospital to give birth to me via an emergency Caesarean section, she had unpacked the tissues and opened them. The top one was pastel-pink instead of its usual white. Nan told her that this was a sign from 'up-above' and that without a doubt

Mum would have her baby girl. Which, of course, she did.

This story might sound a bit silly, but Mum is the Kleenex-Queen! Believe me – she's kept Kleenex in business!

Before that pink tissue was found – and the forty years since – Mum has bought thousands of boxes of tissues, and not once has she found a tissue of any colour in any box.

I think this story illustrates that spirit people are constantly around us, giving us little signs that can take many forms, and can only be judged by the recipient.

For years mediums and psychics have been at the brunt of so many jokes, and their work has not been taken very seriously.

Things are changing – thank God! It seems everywhere you look there are programmes on every sort of paranormal activity imaginable – some very good, some not so good, as they seem to be *more* about the medium than the work they are doing.

As Honrad grumbled recently, *There is far too much ME in MEdiumship, these days. So many insist that they are the 'Most Accurate Medium' or the 'Most Powerful Healer'. Evolved souls know that TRUE power comes from their humbleness and willingness to give their love and compassion unconditionally. Evolved souls know they are only one piece of the puzzle and NOT the whole picture.*

I was quite surprised at this forthright observation. (Yes, spirit guides are also people and are entitled to their opinion.)

He's right though. Mediums *can't* work without the love and co-operation of their spirit friends and helpers. All mediums can do is strive to be the clearest channel as possible.

So many people are now opening up to the reality of the spiritual realms and starting to take small baby-steps towards their own unique journey.

The only advice I can give is; be patient, stay humble, and stay sincere with your motives.

I hope that in my own small way, through my readings and through this book, that I've helped to ignite the 'light' that's in all of us.

I truly wish you the greatest of luck in your own unique journey.

Most importantly... enjoy!